DELHI Light, Shades, Shadows

DELHI Light, Shades, Shadows

DN Chaudhuri

NIYOGI BOOKS

Published by

NIYOGI BOOKS
D-78, Okhla Industrial Area, Phase-I
New Delhi-110 020, India
Tel: 91-11-26816301, 49327000
Fax: 91-11-26810483, 26813830
email: niyogibooks@gmail.com
www.niyogibooks.com

Design: Write Media

ISBN: 978-81-90193-64-1

Year of Publication: 2005
1st reprint: 2006
2nd reprint: 2012

Printed at: Niyogi Offset Pvt. Ltd., New Delhi, India

Foreword

June 21, 2005

Those of us who were in Delhi in the 1940s and '50s tiresomely remind younger people that the city used to be unbelievably beautiful and serene. The skies were clear and one could saunter across wide roads. There was almost no means of public transport, but there were hundreds of bicycles and you could always walk down the pavements. The River Yamuna was in flood after every monsoon, and winter meant dew-drenched grass and the intoxicating fragrance of sweet peas. If you drove out to the rural fringe, you inhaled the smell of cauliflower near Moolchand Hospital and sarson-ka-saag near Chirag Dilli. Summer meant dark afternoons and the dramatic 'loo' which swept across, leaving the evenings deliciously cool. And the joy of sleeping out on charpois under the starry skies.

The famous Number 9 bus took students from Moti Bagh to Delhi University, and by the time it reached Mandi House it was swaying dangerously. Kashmere Gate had two arches, through which our little bus took us, past the sweep of green which was Qudsia Bagh, past the turreted Ludlow Castle, on to Indraprastha College and, skirting the Ridge, to the University, a soothing green and quiet oasis.

North Delhi is Dhruva Chaudhuri territory. From his flat on Nicholson Road, near Mori Gate, he and his brothers and friends walked, cycled or took buses up the Ridge, to Chandni Chowk, the Secretariat, to the far-off monuments. Many of us feel a shock of recognition in reading his account. But few of us would have his special talents – the vivid visual quality which only a gifted photographer can have; the tongue-in-cheek humour of a person who never grows old; the sense of loss or anguish which comes from a generous empathy. What Delhi lost because of Partition is best understood through the specific, through stories about those who left, the houses that

remained empty. There is nothing which can compare with his stark account of the burning city in the terrible days of 1947; of the shock of hearing the announcement of Gandhiji's murder over a crackling home-made radio-set; of the dramatic view – or the lack of view – of the Clock Tower in Chandni Chowk.

It is also the story of a boy growing up (not), going to school, enjoying life on the campus, looking for congenial jobs, getting married... always accompanied by a camera. And, as he grew, so did the city. The journey that began in Nicholson Road continues in a quiet, sparsely-populated Kailash Colony in South Delhi, and then in Mayur Vihar, across the Yamuna, where he swam as a little boy.

It is utterly in character that Dhruva N Chaudhuri celebrates his seventieth birthday by going back to where it all began – to Mori Gate, the Ridge, Civil Lines. And it is again in character, and what a lesson for all of us, that after a life punctured with crises, financial difficulties and some disappointments, he looks back not only with tranquility, but with gratitude, on the riches that Delhi has given him. Here is a recipe for contentment that he offers us – pleasure in the small things of life and the free things that Delhi still offers – monuments, flowering trees, birds and beautiful skyscapes.

Happy reading!

Narayani Gupta

Contents

Part 1

Light

Chapter 1

A Journey into Time

Crossing Yamuna bridge, 1947

A Journey into Time

On the late afternoon of March 31, 1942, the Toofan Express finally rumbled across the old bridge on the Yamuna. Catching the first sight of the Red Fort made us forget every hardship of our journey in a flash

It was a cloudy and dark morning on April 1, 2002, when the 2816 Puri Express pulled out of New Delhi station. Occupying two berths in one of the AC coaches, my wife and I were looking forward to a week-long pilgrimage and a holiday in Orissa, far from the cars, the crowds and the cacophony of Delhi. Our train rushed past the concrete jungle, high and low, on both sides of the railway line, and was soon crossing the new railway bridge on the River Yamuna.

Looking upstream along the river towards Old Delhi, I missed the rise and fall of many curved steel girders of the old bridge, which in 1867 brought the railway to the city of Delhi. The memory of that bridge, near the Red Fort, made me realise that exactly sixty years ago, I, along with my mother and two brothers, had crossed the Yamuna for the first time, while coming from Kolkata to Delhi. On the sunny afternoon of March 31, 1942, I had reached this historic city not for a short visit, but for a stay that spanned the rest of the twentieth century.

You could well say that this has been a journey of a lifetime. For, it brought me both, light and vision. The light to choose my path. And the vision to pursue it.

As the Puri Express rushed past the old yellow vaulted roof of Ghaziabad station, which had originally come up to serve as the rail terminus near Delhi, I remembered the details of our first journey. We had travelled on a famous train, called the Toofan Express. The word 'toofan', of course, refers to the high speed of that particular train. Covering the total distance of the 902 miles between Kolkata and Delhi in just over twenty-four hours, many newcomers to Delhi preferred this train to the prestigious Delhi Mail or, more correctly, the Howrah-Kalka Mail. This mail train usually arrived around eight o'clock in the evening, but, when running late, the arrival time was well past midnight.

In those days, nearly all mail or express trains used to be hauled by heavy steam locomotives of either XP or HP class. Those coal-fired engines, puffing smoke and steam, created such an exciting sound and sight show that every boy worth his name wanted to become an engine driver. I, too, was no exception. At the beginning of any railway journey I would take a loving look at the particular type of engine attached to the train and note down the exact configuration of its wheels.

However, in spite of providing many exciting sights as well as achieving rather high speeds, all steam engines of the last century had a shortcoming. On every journey, long or short, these engines showered coal dust, often burning hot, on all passengers from the regal first class to the humble third. So every passenger, irrespective of the class in which he or she was travelling, emerged from the coach covered with coal dust. They often looked like tar babies straight out of a Brer Rabbit book. The only way to avoid such discomfort, which usually only first-class passengers had, was to wash in the shower-fitted bathrooms attached to the first-class compartment.

Six decades later, sitting in the comfort of the half-empty air-conditioned coach of the Puri Express to Orissa, it was difficult, if not impossible, to imagine some of the hardships that my mother and we three brothers had to endure on our twenty-four-hour journey to Delhi. First of all, owing to the acute shortage of funds, we all, including two male escorts, had to travel in a spartan third-class coach. Ladies, and particularly those with a few children, almost never travelled unescorted.

As my father had to come to Delhi alone at short notice, in order to take up a new job, his family had to be escorted on their train journey by Karali Kanta Biswas, our private tutor and a young attendant, Dhanuk Dhari Mandal. Biswas, who must have been in his early thirties, was a freedom fighter and had spent a long time in a British jail. Under the Government of India rules, he found it difficult to get regular employment in Kolkata, and was all too eager to try his luck in Delhi. As for our other escort, Dhanuk Dhari, he refused to work and stay anywhere else except with our family.

At the time we were leaving Kolkata, serious threats of Japanese aerial bombings, or even an invasion, had made everyone flee the city, and that mass exodus included most of our relatives. The crowd at Howrah station in Kolkata had to be seen to be believed. Those days there was no question of any reservation in third-class coaches and compartments. They had only wooden benches and were always overflowing, well above their maximum limits. With the mass exodus from Kolkata in early 1942, every single seat as well as all upper bunks, meant strictly for the luggage, swarmed with men, women and screaming children rushing out from the threatened city.

I still recall, vividly, how the scene in our third-class coach resembled the terrible train journey to Siberia, described in the famous novel *Dr Zhivago* by Boris Pasternak, and also depicted just as vividly in the film directed by David Lean. Unlike in the janta or people's coaches running today, there was not a single fan that could be found anywhere in the third-class coaches of the forties. That, and the overcrowding in our train, made our journey to Delhi a great ordeal, particularly when we had to cross the arid landscape of Uttar Pradesh.

The other problem while travelling in a train, particularly during the summer months, happened to be the incessant demand for drinking water from everyone, young and old. Looking at a chilled bottle of mineral water glistening on a side table in the Puri Express, I could not help remembering how, in the past, all drinking water had to be carried either in earthen pitchers, or metal water bottles covered with khaki felt. Even then, unless clamped in wooden stands, the pitchers would invariably roll over with every possible jolt of the train, spilling their content at the very start of a long journey. In contrast, supplies from water bottles, though comparatively secure, were always in short supply, and every possible drop had to be rationed till the arrival at an important station. Once there, a stampede usually started towards the all-too-scarce water taps of that station. The scene there usually resembled an African waterhole, a shot often used in wildlife films on television.

Food was generally served by our ever-caring mother straight from a tiffin carrier, which used to be often packed with luchis or puris made with white flour, accompanied by aloo dum or potato curry. Dry sandesh made with milk always got preference over other messy sweets such as rasgollas. However, for the main meals on long distance trains, dining cars and refreshment rooms, both vegetarian and non-vegetarian, were run by foreign companies such as Kellnar's or Spencer's. Those railway caterers served food and drinks of such excellent quality and in such great style, that their meal services would have put to shame the Rajdhani first-class services of today.

On our journey to Delhi on the Toofan Express, we had two servings of multi-course meals served to us on the second day, in our ordinary third-class compartment. Those ample and delicious lunches, each worth about a rupee for a plate, satisfied all of us – except Dhanuk Dhari. He refused to touch anything cooked in an unknown kitchen and served by a person, who though looked grand in his achkan and turban, might have been an alien from another community. Dhanu, as we called him, used to get down at one of the big stations such as Allahabad or Kanpur to stuff himself with freshly fried puris and bhajji. This was prepared right in front of him, at the platform, by the ever-present Brahmin Panditji, who wielded a ladle over a smoking kadhai while frying an endless supply of hot puris.

So far my description of the long train journey to Delhi in the early forties might give the impression that it was all a struggle and there was no fun. But that was not so. I have already mentioned the enjoyable railroad fare, always welcome after the usual dose of healthy but dull home-cooked meals. Further, the polished green appearance of every train on the Eastern Indian Railway (EIR) line was enough to create an impression of smartness and order, which have all but disappeared in practically every train of today, except probably in the Rajdhani and Shatabdi.

In those days of comparatively safe rail travel, the windows and doors had no traces of iron bars or darkened glasses. So the wide world going past those windows created an ever-changing pattern of a kaleidoscope. As a bonus, whenever a passenger train steamed into a station, there was this enchanting audiovisual show presented by platform vendors, including the ubiquitous chai walla and magazine hawkers. All this has now been dimmed and silenced by the dark and sealed windows of the all-too-comfortable AC coaches. Even in the non-AC coaches of today, the profusion of iron bars and grills, though necessary, always create an impression of a prison cell, or sitting on the wrong side of a fence in a zoological park.

On our first long journey to Delhi we enjoyed many interesting sights such as the horse-drawn vehicles, tongas and ekkas, as well as less common camel carts. Such a profusion of animal-drawn vehicles could never be seen in Kolkata. Also, we could see a whole range of birds such as green bee-eaters, black drongos as well as kingfishers and bluejays or neel kanth, cavorting on telegraph wires all along the railway lines. Sadly, on this rail journey, while going east, there was practically no trace of such wonderful birds.

On the late afternoon of March 31, 1942, the Toofan Express finally rumbled across the old bridge on the Yamuna. Catching the first sight of the Red Fort, along with its marble pavilions topped by chhatris, all gleaming white, made us forget every hardship of our journey in a flash. Soon after crossing the bridge next to the fort of Salimgarh, all of us were excited to catch a fleeting glimpse of the great Jama Masjid towering over the old city of Delhi.

Little did I realise, then, that this city was going to be my home. A home that would provide me an opportunity to chronicle its growth, as well as mine, with the help of my camera, the tool of my chosen profession. The light, shades and shadows of this changing city would be captured in my mind's eye, as well as in countless rolls of film. After going past rows of goods wagons as well as a few steam engines hissing in the yard, our train entered one of the six platforms of Delhi junction. There, at the very beginning of that platform, stood my

■ Shahjahanabad, 1953

Qutb Minar, 1956

father, rather conspicuous in a grey tropical suit, complete with a blue silk tie and a felt hat. Looking at him, no one could ever imagine that he was dressed in his very first suit, which he got made only a week before his arrival in Delhi. In contrast, his entire family and the two male escorts, after that tough rail journey, looked definitely plebian and grubby.

The year 1942 had started on quite a difficult note for my father who, almost ten years later, was to become the illustrious 'Unknown Indian' after writing his autobiography. Before coming to Delhi he had been working in Kolkata as the private secretary to Sarat Chandra Bose, an eminent nationalist leader, and the elder brother of Netaji Subhas Chandra Bose. It is believed that Netaji had escaped under the very eye of the Kolkata police in 1941 and he had managed to reach Germany and then, finally, Japan to fight the British.

However, at No 1, Woodburn Park, the palatial three-storeyed residence of Sarat Chandra Bose, which also happened to be my father's office in Kolkata, there were no signs of outward trouble. As our house was located at a nearby locality of Bhowanipur, my younger brother and I often went down to Woodburn Park to play with Sarat Bose's younger children.

Then, on an apparent calm evening of December 12, 1941, five days after the Japanese air force had attacked Pearl Harbour, Sarat Chandra Bose was arrested from his house. As chance would have it, we were playing in the garden that very evening. All of a sudden we saw a car with an English officer entering the main house. Within minutes an ominous dark shadow seemed to have fallen on that huge mansion and our playmates were immediately called in. Feeling rather lost and confused, we tried to locate our father when a tall and thin Muslim gentleman, who appeared to be Fazlul Huq, an important political figure of undivided Bengal, asked us gently to get lost. We rushed home, unescorted, to inform our mother that all was not well at Woodburn Park. Soon our father returned home for his early dinner and, after confirming the disturbing news, mentioned rather casually that he would no longer be going to his office at Woodburn Park.

Father used to broadcast talks on current affairs regularly from the Kolkata station of the All India Radio, and that had been his source of another reasonable income. But, one day in February 1942, he came back after his usual broadcast and seemed to be rather upset and pensive. Soon my mother was told that there had been an exchange of strong words with the controller of the All India Radio and all his income from the All India Radio would probably cease. One of the reasons for this confrontation was an article in which my father had been rather critical of certain wartime policies of the All India Radio. Added to these financial difficulties, the constant threat of Japanese air attacks and the imposition of a blackout in Kolkata created a sombre mood in our family. Then, one afternoon in the last week of February, Father got an offer for a regular job at the News Services Division of the All India Radio in Delhi. So, after a few weeks of negotiations, and getting his first set of European clothes made, he left Kolkata, as it turned out, for good. Little did he know that he was destined to complete an unbeaten century of his life at the university town of Oxford situated in his beloved England.

The journey in time continues. Memories keep rushing by. We are heading for Delhi on the last day of March in 1942 and I have a fairly vivid recollection of the scene on a platform of Delhi junction. There were suitcases, trunks and several rolls of bedding called hold-alls scattered all around. Also, there were a couple of tiffin carriers and thermos flasks, which were necessary for carrying food and milk required for a journey with three young boys, among whom the youngest was not yet three. As if that was not enough, just before we started for Delhi, Father had cabled Mother not to leave behind his extensive record collection of music by Bach, Beethoven and Mozart, along with a hand-wound gramophone fitted with an exponential horn.

In addition, there on the platform stood a full-size reproduction of Leonardo's *Mona Lisa*, propped up against our formidable-looking gramophone. While leaving the railway station with so much luggage, my mother, as well as our main escort Karali Babu, had to face a rather sticky situation at the exit of the Delhi junction.

All this while, father stood haughtily aloof with only our baby brother in his arms, and when our final marching orders came, we two elder brothers, aged seven and nine, trotted out of the railway station, clutching a small suitcase between us. That battered suitcase contained among our various toys a shiny box camera worth five-and-a-half rupees.

Sixty years later, as the Puri Express shot past Aligarh, Hathras and other towns of Uttar Pradesh, I still could not believe how that little camera, along with the historic city of Delhi, had shaped my life.

Chapter 2

The View from Above

Kashmere Gate, 1946

The View from Above

The scene from our front verandah appeared to be straight out of an eighteenth-century colour engraving by Daniells. The city beckoned us young and enthusiastic boys, with its promise of adventure, fun and hope

The big clock on the portico of Delhi junction showed a few minutes past five when we stepped out of the railway station. Almost immediately a platoon of tonga wallas, nearly all with their huge turbans and flowing beards, surrounded us to begin a fierce battle of words as well as gestures to capture this group of newcomers as passengers. After a good deal of haggling and jostling with our pile of luggage, we finally left the station building, which was certainly an impressive piece of Victorian Gothic architecture.

As we clip-clopped in a convoy of three tongas down Queen's Road of Old Delhi, we saw one of the two important boulevards running parallel to the railway line, which had divided the old city into two. Shortly after crossing the railway line over Dufferin Bridge, our horse-drawn vehicles reached an area known as Mori Gate and turned into a road called Nicholson Road. This particular road ran all along the old city wall of Shahjahanabad and right next to the old wall was our house in the P&O Building.

Within a few days of his arrival, Father had managed to find a spacious flat on the top floor of the P&O Building, which was located within an easy walking distance from his office in Civil Lines. Rather than move into that residential accommodation alone, he had asked Mother to come to Delhi with all of us at the earliest possible date. About a year later, when the All India Radio finally shifted its office and studios to the new broadcasting house on Parliament Street, and official quarters were offered to us, my parents refused to move from our flat in Old Delhi. They continued to stay in Mori Gate for almost thirty years till they left for England in 1970. While I, on my part, lived there till the early sixties, and, only after getting married, moved on to a new colony in South Delhi.

Our flat on Nicholson Road was on the top floor of the P&O Building, which stood at the corner of the main Nicholson Road and a narrow lane. A dark and steep staircase, typical of most houses of Old Delhi, climbed up from that lane to our flat; we began to call it Humayun's staircase. This peculiar name was derived from the well-known story of Mughal Emperor Humayun who fell to his death on the steep and dark staircase at Purana Qila.

After going up that staircase, when we finally reached our flat, high above the old wall, we had a magnificent view of the entire Civil Lines and also Kashmere Gate. On the very first evening of our arrival, after eating some oily snacks bought from a local sweet shop, we rushed out to the front verandah and marvelled at the view of the setting sun beyond the tree line of Tis Hazari Maidan. Right in front, after a curtain of green neem and peepul trees, stood the Northern Ridge. And there, through a gap in the thick foliage of trees, we could see the old ruin of Pir Ghaib, which was once the hunting lodge of Feroz Shah Tughlaq.

We were rather excited to know that in the fourteenth century, when Pir Ghaib was built, lions often roamed in the scrubland around this particular area. Lions had been last sighted in Haryana near Delhi as late as 1827 by Charles Trevelyan, the young Deputy Commissioner.

To our right, the old city wall, which stretched up to Kashmere Gate, was glowing under the last rays of the evening sun. The scene from our front verandah appeared to be straight out of an eighteenth-century colour engraving by Daniells. The city beckoned us young and enthusiastic boys, with its promise of adventure, fun and hope.

We fell asleep early that night on improvised beds with the sound of peacocks from the distant Ridge, and a few jackals howling away in the thickets of Civil Lines. After being used to the urban atmosphere of Kolkata, certainly the evening ambience around our new residence at Mori Gate was both, strange and somewhat uncanny.

Next morning, soon after dawn, we were woken by a series of three religious sounds, which were rather symbolic of the three successive empires in Delhi. The first sound to greet our ears was the constant clanging of metal bells and gongs, mixed with the sound of more than one conch shell. This early sound of morning worship came from a temple, which happened to be the first Bengali Kali Bari or Kali temple of

Delhi. The second sound, which floated in that morning, was a long drawn out azaan from an old mosque near Mori Gate. After a while, we heard the distant peal of a church bell, which came from the St. James' Church at Kashmere Gate. The legacy of the British rule in 1942 was further reinforced by more than one bugle call from the police lines just across the old wall.

Later, when the sun had risen well above Kashmere Gate, my brother and I rushed out of the confines of the city wall and began to explore the area just outside Mori Gate. Though called a gate, Mori Gate was only an opening in the city wall. The main gate was actually demolished, along with Kabul Gate and Lahore Gate, by the newly-founded Municipality of Delhi in the late nineteenth century and, unlike Kashmere Gate, was never rebuilt.

After coming out of Mori Gate, we first moved along a moat running outside the old wall of Shahjahanabad. Within a short distance of about a hundred yards, we came across a round bastion called Martello Tower, which had been erected by a British engineer, and also carried his name. Instead of going further towards Kashmere Gate, we decided to retrace our steps to a roundabout with a statue of a soldier just outside Mori Gate. The statue was that of a British army engineer called Captain Alexander Taylor who had helped General Nicholson attack the old city in September 1857. All around Taylor's statue were pygmy iron mortars pointing towards a square bastion called Mori Bastion and, a little further, was the spot where Nicholson was shot fatally. Earlier there used to be a statue of General Nicholson, sword in hand, at the centre of a park called Nicholson Park, a short distance outside Mori Gate.

Sitting astride those little mortars at the roundabout outside Mori Gate we could see, rising right above the old wall, a long row of new buildings; this included the name of our house, P&O Building. This curious name was written boldly on a triangular pediment on the roof and had nothing to do with the famous shipping line of that age. The initials stood for Percy and Oswald, who were the two sons of the owner of our building, Julie Pinto. She was an elderly Christian lady from the coastal town of Mangalore.

This custom of naming buildings after their owners or relatives was a common practice in that area of Old Delhi. Hasan Building, Rashid Building, Afzal Mansion implied that those buildings belonged to Muslims. On the other hand, Hari Ram Building or Bhupendra Bhawan

■ Old wall near Mori Gate, 1953

had owners who were obviously Hindus. Though, during the Mughal times, many areas around Mori Gate were considered poor, some of those buildings, which had come up in the thirties on Nicholson Road, belonged to well-to-do merchants or retired government officials from different communities. They usually occupied a flat or two, according to the size of their families, and let out the rest of the accommodation to those preferably from their own community. There was, for instance, an Anglo-Indian owner who had retired from the Railways. He would always prefer to let out his flats to tenants whose names were distinctly English, such as Rightman, Fallows or even Alexander. Notable exceptions were, however, Bengalis, who worked mostly for the government and ate fish and rice.

Our locality on Nicholson Road was not a traditional locality of Old Delhi. It was rather cosmopolitan in character. Here, in many of the residential flats and houses, well-to-do Hindu as well as Muslim families lived in perfect harmony with Parsi, Christian and even Jewish families. Though there was very little social interaction among these communities, on festive days, after making discreet inquiries regarding the acceptance of eatables, sweets such as laddoos, halwas and cakes, all home-made, were exchanged along with the customary dry and fresh fruits.

The building just opposite ours, across the narrow lane, had a large flat on the first floor. Like a typical first-floor flat of that locality, it had many rooms around a central courtyard and a wide verandah in front. Owing to its size as well as the privacy it offered, this particular flat had been occupied by a Nawab from an estate in Uttar Pradesh. This elderly Nawab used to commute often between his estate and this flat, which was usually occupied by a part of his large family.

Rather unusually, he would do this trip in his own horse-drawn cart. Whenever we saw a tonga tilted backwards on its two wheels, as well as horses munching dry grass under an alcove of the old wall, we knew that the Nawab had come to Delhi. Among his retinue was an Afghan guard with flowing robes and a fearsome black beard. This 'Kabuliwalla', as we called him, went about with a monkey on his shoulder and, during his evening walks, entertained us with the antics of his pet as well as stories of his journey to Delhi.

The senior Begum Sahiba happened to be quite a formidable lady owing both, to her size as well as her voice. Also, she did not care very much about observing purdah once inside her flat. Right from the beginning of the summer season she would be sleeping on a bedstead made of solid silver that was placed at a spot in the verandah that had the maximum breeze.

She had a Eurasian girl to attend to her personal needs. But, what appeared to be even more surprising was her constant habit of smoking a silver hookah decorated with rich Bidri work. As she talked, her voice appeared to be a deep contralto if not tenor and, when all of a sudden she shouted an order for a freshly charged hookah, it sounded like an officer of the guards calling, "Attention!"

This formidable lady had several young girls around her. They could have been her daughters or even granddaughters. Two of them studied at Indraprastha College, the oldest women's college of Delhi. They were always covered in burqas and even their college bus was like a prison van. The windows of that vehicle not only had iron bars for good security but were also covered with a thick wire mesh. All these dark, protective covers further heightened the mystery of the constant giggles and chatter that would emanate from the interiors of that vehicle.

I had never seen a bus like that before, nor a burqa-clad woman for that matter. So one morning, when I was returning home after buying bread and butter at a shop, called Mullaji's, and saw that strangely built bus standing right before our house, my curiosity got the better of me and I began to examine the college bus with keen interest. Within minutes, two of the college girls, covered in burqas, began to walk up to their vehicle. Suddenly, one of the girls threw up the visor of her burqa and, after making a face at me, jumped into the dark interiors of her bus. I was flabbergasted, to say the least, and raced up to our flat. But once there, I was greeted with a verbal bashing from my mother who had seen the whole episode from the balcony. It was difficult indeed to explain to her that my interest was only in the curiously built college transport of Indraprastha College.

Moving on from the old to the new, or rather from the Mughal to the British. There was this newly married Parsi couple who stayed next door, only a floor above Nawab Sahib's flat. Young Mr and Mrs Sidhwa were a friendly lot like many people from their community and often took us, the two elder brothers, out for shopping as well as for watching cricket, which used to be played on a lush green lawn outside Mori Gate. On all these excursions Mrs Sidhwa usually wore a Parsi saree with a rich floral border. But sometimes, on Saturday afternoons, while visiting Apollo Hotel, she would be dressed in smart European clothes. She looked like a picture straight out of a popular ladies journal called *Woman and Home*.

Apollo Hotel, on Nicholson Road, was more or less like an English pub for the Parsi community. It had a signboard with 'Bar & Billiard' written boldly above the entrance. The main doorway had a pair of swing doors that blocked the view of the lounge quite effectively. This lack of vision, along with the mystery about the activities proclaimed outside Apollo Hotel, further heightened our curiosity.

Then, one Saturday afternoon, after a shopping trip around Kashmere Gate, my brother and I got an unexpected chance to have this mystery of 'Bar & Billiard' unravelled once and for all. On our way back from Kashmere Gate, Mr Sidhwa suddenly decided to play a game of snooker with a friend at Apollo Hotel. Once inside he ordered chilled draught beer for himself and his friend. Mrs Sidhwa and we two brothers sipped orange squash, sitting inside a nearby lounge, imbibing the distinct English ambience.

General Nicholson's statue, 1946

Unlike many of the houses in our neighbourhood in Kolkata, almost all ground floors on Nicholson Road were business premises. In our building, for example, Mrs Pinto owned a thriving printing press and, soon after we moved in, she installed a huge Heidelberg machine in order to print some of the large war posters in three colours. At times, the deep rumble of that machine was enough to keep us wide awake at night.

There were three automobile repair shops on our road and, along with cars such as the Austin, Morris and Chevrolet, we saw a steady stream of exotic looking cars such as the Jaguar, MG, Cadillac and even a Rolls Royce. One day, when a Lagonda Cabriolet of 1920 or 1925 vintage appeared with its pneumatic horn shaped like a snake, we just had to rush down to the street below to have a closer look.

There was another small factory on Nicholson Road that had been of great interest to us as well as to the many adults who wanted to add a little pep to their lives. This was an ice cream-cum-aerated water factory. We would often go in and watch how carbon dioxide was compressed manually into bottles of soda water and lemonade. Aerated water bottles in those days had solid glass balls as stoppers to keep the drinks sparkling. Sometimes, such bottles were snatched from a corner paan or beetle leaf shop and used as explosive missiles in street fights or riots among rival groups. In August 1942, we witnessed a major political upheaval around Mori Gate where such bottles made up for the lack of bombs and hand grenades in a crowd of fighters.

One evening, shortly after our arrival in Delhi, it happened to be my father's weekly holiday, and I was sent to a newspaper office-cum-press near Mori Gate. The name of that paper, if I recall correctly, was *The National Call*. A few years later it became *The Morning Chronicle*, and was finally taken over by *The Indian Express* group. That particular day in April 1942, Sir Stafford Cripps, an important minister in the British cabinet, was flying into New Delhi with an offer of 'Dominion Status' for India. For my father to wait till the next morning for his usual newspaper was next to impossible. So there I was, waiting at the doorstep of *The National Call* printing press, and I finally saw the evening edition rolling out with a picture of Stafford Cripps getting down from an aeroplane at Willingdon Airport, next to Safdarjung's Tomb. However, the excitement and also the expectation that was created by the British minister's visit were extremely short-lived. Mahatma Gandhi, along with other Indian leaders, called the offer a post-dated cheque of doubtful value. Then, one night, when Father returned home after his evening broadcast, he mentioned that he had actually seen Sir Stafford Cripps in person at the news studio of the All India Radio. He was rather surprised by the amiable expression on the British minister's face that evening.

For the next few months our life around Mori Gate went on smoothly, except for the unfamiliar dry heat of Delhi. On the top-floor flat of the P&O Building all of us had to face the full fury of the heat and dust of the Delhi summer, which turned the landscape as well as the sky into a shade of morbid yellow. Further, to add to the acute discomfort of that summer heat, there was not a single fan in our flat. This absence of fans in a reasonably well-to-do family like ours had been because of my father's esoteric view about the Indian summer. One evening, after some weeks of sweltering weather and sleepless nights, we suddenly saw dark clouds rolling in from the east, and soon a heavy pre-monsoon shower changed the atmosphere around Mori Gate completely.

From the crack of dawn, hundreds of Muslim women completely covered in white as well as black burqas began to pour out of the opening in the Mori Gate wall and proceed towards the Yamuna through Qudsia Garden. They were accompanied by dozens of children fluttering around them like busy bees. On monsoon days the men folk usually took it easy and went over to either Okhla or Qutb Minar with musical instruments and portable gramophones.

Then from August 9, 1942 onwards, after the 'Quit India' call was given by Mahatma Gandhi, there were signs of serious trouble all over India. On a pleasant morning, we saw more than one platoon of British soldiers with rifles and light machine guns gathering on the lawns outside the old city. Within minutes they began to get into battle formations and pointed their rifles and machine guns towards the opening in the old wall. Though no actual action was visible or heard that morning, we did feel that all was not well in Delhi.

A little later, these soldiers, with their officers' and NCOs' barking orders, trooped through Mori Gate to stage a flag march all over the old city. Late that evening we came to know that important Congress leaders all over India, including Mahatma Gandhi and Pandit Nehru, had been arrested and sent to various jails in obscure Indian towns.

From the next day hell broke loose throughout India. Shortly after lunchtime, we went upstairs to get a first-hand look. What we did see from that high vantage point of our house was really stunning. A multi-storeyed office of the Railways, called Peeli Kothi, was going up in flames, and within an interval of less than twenty minutes it collapsed like a raging inferno. More than half-a-century later, when I saw the World Trade Centre in New York collapsing on television, I was reminded of my childhood. Even today, the burnt shell of that Railway office can be seen at the end of Queen's Road.

The Quit India Movement of 1942 had repercussions which affected us considerably. After coming to Delhi we were always delighted to ride trolley buses that were regularly running between Tis Hazari and Tirpolia Gate, beyond the old Sabzi Mandi. Those unique electric buses with rubber-tyred wheels could easily move in through the crowded locality of Sabzi Mandi. They were burnt down in 1942, and the service wound up.

My childhood is inextricably woven with these enchanting streets of Old Delhi. It was here that I spent some of my most unforgettable moments. The sounds and light of that city remain with me even today.

Chapter 3

Stones and Streets of Old Delhi

Red Fort, 1954

Stones and Streets of Old Delhi

In those days a large number of birds such as hoopoes, parrots and woodpeckers could be seen among the many trees and gardens of the Red Fort. The comparison between the real birds along with those depicted on the throne canopy of Diwan-e-Aam was a game that we really enjoyed playing

Soon after our teacher Mr Biswas left Delhi, my father decided that we, his two elder boys, should be given a chance to see and learn about the historical monuments in the Seven Cities of Delhi. One of my uncles, who had been very close to our family in Kolkata, had also come to Delhi on his annual Durga Puja holiday, and was keen to visit the old sites scattered all over this city. So my father thought that an excursion to the Red Fort as well as the Jama Masjid should not be put off later than the next day, which happened to be his weekly holiday.

Even though the prevalent weather over Delhi had turned somewhat mild during those early autumn days, the Red Fort was given a clear preference over the distant Qutb Minar on account of its proximity to Mori Gate. Also, some sweets and other delicacies had to be purchased for the coming Puja festival. However, though excited at the prospect of this educational excursion, we had some stiff mental hurdles to cross before that interesting trip. Right from early morning we had to learn all the important facts about the Red Fort, including the date of its completion in 1648. Next, we had to pronounce correctly all the names such as Qila-i-Mu'alla (Exalted Fort), along with the other landmarks, Naqqar Khana, Nahar-i-Bihisht, as well as the real tongue-twisting Musamman Burj. While this chant about the Red Fort was going on like the mini version of an Urdu madrassa, Father suddenly disappeared from our flat, telling my mother that he would return soon. He also added in his characteristic way that his breakfast of soft-boiled rice and an egg along with some vegetables should have no trace of green chilies. We were rather happy on getting this unexpected break from memorising the facts and figures about the Red Fort, and decided to rush to the terrace with a pair of old opera glasses. Once there, our intention was to take a good look at Lahore Gate of the Red Fort as well as the Jama Masjid, rising above the old city of Shahjahanabad, and visible from the rooftop.

After half-an-hour we saw our father again, with three slim books bought from a small bookshop located near Mori Gate. The first of those books was H Sharp's *Delhi: Its Story and Buildings*. The others were official guidebooks on the Red Fort and the Qutb Minar, and were published by the Archaeological Survey of India at an unbelievable price of one rupee per volume. At that point in time we were rather young to go through Sharp's *Delhi*, but what we found to be of great interest were the guidebooks with large aerial drawings of the Red Fort and the Qutb enclosure at Mehrauli. Soon, we memorised those drawings like a crew of pilots and navigators about to fly into unfamiliar territory.

Around three in the afternoon we, along with our uncle, who spoke very little Hindi but lent us solid moral support with his physical size, went across to an archaic tonga stand for our afternoon trip. The fare for that entire excursion, including a stop at Chandni Chowk for buying sweets, was fixed at about twelve annas or less than a rupee. Then, with the sun well past the meridian, all of us managed to troop into the majestic Lahore Gate, and stood under the shade of that barbican, which was built by Mughal Emperor Aurangzeb. While two able-bodied British sentries armed with 303 rifles guarded the main entrance of the Red Fort, a Union Jack was seen fluttering prominently above Lahore Gate. Those soldiers and the colourful flag in red, blue and white proclaimed the British rule over India in no uncertain terms.

All of a sudden, the blonde head of an English woman appeared out of a window high above Lahore Gate, and with her hands she gestured to us in an impatient manner to move off from that spot immediately. The elderly lady seemed to be clearly upset by the above average pitch and decibel of my father's voice, while he was elaborating to us the story of Shah Jahan's distress at the addition of a stone veil to his beloved Urdu-i-Mu'alla, the original name of the Red Fort. Of course, it was rather a critical time for the British Empire in India, and I suppose no English man or woman felt quite secure while living in the old city. So instead of waiting further and inviting trouble we just moved into the Chhatta Chowk arcade of the Lahore Gate. Chhatta Chowk or the Mina Bazaar of Shah

Jahan's palace was once a colourful market and even sixty years ago there were many shops reminiscent of the Mughal times. They sold everything from curios such as miniature paintings on ivory to edibles such as parathas, kababs and ice cream. Also, both hot and cold drinks such as tea and lemonade were available in plenty. As we walked down that covered bazaar, many of the shopkeepers standing in their traditional dress of achkans and astrakhan caps implored us to step into their shops and examine their exquisite wares. All along Chhatta Chowk their clamour in chaste Urdu was rather loud. It went a long way to create an atmosphere of the elegant Mughal times.

But on stepping out of the cloistered area of Chhatta Chowk the atmosphere changed in a flash – from the polite Mughal era to the harsh reality of the British rule. As we were walking up to Naqqar Khana, or the Drum Pavilion, there were signboards everywhere with crude caricatures of men behind bars, being whipped, or even hanged, to frighten the poor Indian public from straying into the area under the control of the British troupes. Also, the constant rushing around of military vehicles, including armoured cars with mounted machine guns, added to this discordant note. However, after crossing the narrow iron-gate of Naqqar or Nahabat Khana, the atmosphere around the Red Fort once again turned serene. At this particular spot, during the days of the Mughal rule, everyone except the Emperor and his favourite son had to dismount from his horse or elephant and walk to the grandiose Diwan-e-Aam of the palace. During the reign of King Bahadur Shah, the last Mughal Emperor, an Englishman called Hawkins refused to observe this etiquette and rode right up to Diwan-e-Khas on a horse, accompanied by a friend. Even though the king himself was not present in the palace, taking such liberties inside the Red Fort as Hawkins did was noted very seriously, and he was removed from his prestigious job of the Resident, the de facto ruler of Delhi.

Naqqar Khana or the Drum Pavilion was a beautiful pavilion made of red sandstone with floral carvings all over the exterior wall facing the Diwan-e-Aam. From the top of this charming building a band of royal pipers and drummers used to herald the many hours of the day, and also the arrival as well as the departure of the king. Curiously enough, on that very first visit, as well as on other subsequent visits, we noticed a portly looking Englishman, dressed in khaki shorts and a bold check shirt, complete with a pipe clinched between his teeth, moving in and around Naqqar Khana. We came to know that he was an official from the Archaeological Survey of India who looked after the historical portion of the Fort. He appeared scholarly and rather mild. This was in complete contrast with the churlish and generally loud British soldiers who swarmed all around the Red Fort.

On stepping onto the main historical area and entering the red pavilion of the Diwan-e-Aam, we approached the marble throne canopy decorated with rich pietra-dura panels. There was no restriction on climbing that canopy. This enabled us to get a detailed view of the marble wall with coloured stone panels depicting many varieties of birds, flowers and an image of Orpheus playing the lute.

In those days a large number of birds such as hoopoes, parrots and woodpeckers could be seen among the many trees and gardens of the Red Fort. The comparison between the real birds along with those depicted on the throne canopy of Diwan-e-Aam was a game that we really enjoyed playing. It was rather interesting to know from my father, an avid anglophile, that the entire pietra-dura panel, including the image of Orpheus, was brought back from Kensington Museum, London, by the Viceroy Lord Curzon at his own expense. After coming down from the throne platform through a staircase meant exclusively for the rulers of the Red Fort, we had the choice of either proceeding towards the zenana quarter, now represented by the solitary pavilion of the Rang Mahal, or like the privileged few of the Mughal era, to the defunct Lal Purdah Darwaza or the red curtain doorway.

This arched doorway with a red felt curtain admitted a limited number of people to the hall of private audience, the Diwan-e-Khas, and to the nearby Khas Mahal, the private apartment of the Emperor. At this point of our exploration, we were rather surprised with the lack of doors and privacy in almost all the buildings of this royal abode. However, there was one room in Khas Mahal that had two ornate metal doors. On one of our subsequent visits we found one of those doors open and were able to look in.

It was a room decorated in an original Mughal way, including a royal hookah and a sword. Next to this door was the baithak, or the sitting room, with the translucent marble screen designed with the scale of justice along with two swords.

Coming back to this enchanting afternoon, when we entered the Diwan-e-Khas more than one local guide pounced upon us to read the famous couplet, 'Agar firdaus barni-i-zamin ast, Hamin ast...' (loosely translated: If there is Paradise on earth, it is here...).

The Diwan-e-Khas had nothing extraordinary to offer after the interesting lotus fountain and the dry, but visible, water channel called Nahar-i-Bihisht inside the Rang Mahal. This colourful pavilion of the principal begum was mainly used as a purdah, or cloistered common room. The reigning king usually had all his meals in this pavilion on a dastarkhan spread over sheets of stretched leather that covered the costly carpet.

Moving on to the hamam or the bathing chamber, we saw the intricate hot-and-cold water arrangements as well as the marble floor with rich floral decorations. Finally, after reaching Shah Burj at the last corner of the Red Fort, we could see the forbidden Salimgarh across Bela Road, and also the two-storeyed railway bridge painted bright red. All along the Yamuna we noticed many bundles of freshly cut logs floating from forests upstream.

After looking at the lovely Hayat Bakh garden with its idyllic pavilions called Sawan and Bhadon, we felt more at ease on leaving behind those multi-storeyed stone barracks that were packed with Britishers shouting and laughing at Indian visitors, particularly women. We came

Rang Mahal, Red Fort, 1955

across an isolated pavilion called Mumtaz or Sheesh Mahal. This building in Mughal times had really been an annex to Rang Mahal. After the British occupation, the building was used as a prison for errant soldiers. It had been turned into a museum of great interest. Here we could see curious objects such as jade plates and bowls, which were supposed to crack if any trace of poison had been present in the food meant for the royal consumer. Among the wide range of weapons and arms displayed, there were two swords that belonged to Emperors Shah Jahan and Aurangzeb. At the same museum there was a rich collection of paintings and engravings on display, and these pictures in full colour gave a clear idea about the life and activities inside the palaces.

And, among all these paintings and engravings, we suddenly came across an original photograph, yellowed with age. It depicted the last Mughal Emperor, Bahadur Shah Zafar, reclining on a bed, probably during the time when he had been imprisoned in two dingy rooms at the fringe of his own palace. It was indeed sad to see the deposed king holding on to the pipe of his hookah as a last resort to comfort. At that time the Emperor was more than eighty, and it is perhaps an irony of fate that in the Diwan-e-Khas itself, where he once ruled supreme, all the British judges held him guilty for allowing many atrocities inside the Red Fort. Finally, he was banished to the distant town of Rangoon, along with his queen Zinat Mahal and some other members of his family.

Though there were no photographs of Zinat Mahal that could be seen, she was well represented by more than one painting as well as a set of her attire. In our boyhood days we had taken the revealing design of that dress as something of a historical fact, but one of my aunts visiting Delhi in 1945 was so offended with Zinat Mahal's dress that she walked out of Sheesh Mahal as well as the Red Fort. It was probably fortunate that she died a good decade before the coming of the satellite and cable television to India.

All the buildings, including the little Moti Masjid built by Aurangzeb, had a picturesque and tranquil look. There was no indication of the turmoil and misery that went on inside the Red Fort at the time of the Mughal rule, especially after Aurangzeb.

In spite of a grand façade of pomp and splendour inside the Red Fort, all forms of intrigue and violence continued unabated for more than a century. Often rulers of Delhi such as Emperor

Shah Alam were blinded and deposed from the throne. Many queens, such as Hazrat Qudsia Begum of Qudsia Bagh's fame, usually took an active part in all forms of palace intrigue, while hidden behind a latticed screen.

These political intrigues and family feuds among the rulers in Delhi became apparent to the foreign visitors who came to the Mughal court in Delhi. One such visitor happened to be Bishop Heber from Kolkata who, during his extensive travel, recorded all that he saw in and around Delhi. When Bishop Heber called on Emperor Akbar Shah II in1824, he noticed that many areas of the Red Fort, including the Diwan-i-Aam, had become quite dingy and the areas were dirty with pigeon and bat droppings. There were slums inhabited by royal descendants called salatin.

Two early photographs of the Red Fort taken by a European photographer called Felice Beato in 1858 support this statement. Though most of the living quarters and other buildings inside the Red Fort had been demolished by the British army, we should be grateful to Lord Curzon, the Viceroy of India, not only for saving the fort from further vandalism and destruction, but also for restoring its pristine glory. Our exit from the Red Fort was through the other gate called Delhi Gate. Once there, we could see two stone elephants symbolically guarding the archway with huge doors covered with anti-elephant spikes. Since it was rather late to visit the Jama Masjid at that hour of maghreb or evening prayers, we got into our tonga after walking along the deep moat.

When we rode into Chandni Chowk the entire market had begun to glitter with lights. After the total blackout conditions of Kolkata streets it was good to see the jeweller's lane called Dariba Kalan, glittering like a bride.

At a short distance from that lane we noticed a towering gurudwara called Sis Gunj. It was built on a site where the Sikh Guru Teg Bahadur was tortured to death by Aurangzeb. On the steps of that imposing shrine stood two Nihang Sikh guards looking magnificent in their blue and yellow turbans and formidable lances. Just next to the gurudwara was the Kotwali or the main police station of Delhi. This infamous place had been active right from the Mughal days and, once again, we saw a Union Jack being taken down the tall flagpole after the sounding of the last post for that day in 1942.

There, right in front of the Kotwali, was a well-known square of Old Delhi called the Fountain.

■ Sweet shop, Chandni Chowk, 1952

At the far end of this Square was the medical chamber and pharmacy of a pioneer Bengali doctor, HC Sen, who, apart from treating poor people for a negligible sum, kept an open house for all Bengali visitors to Delhi till 1912. Later, the British Commissioner had to ask the Sen family to curtail their hospitality because many Bengali revolutionaries were taking advantage of this free shelter available in Delhi.

Our tonga stopped near the Fountain Square just under a tiny mosque with three golden domes. This mosque, known as the Chhota Sunehri Masjid, had quite a sad history. It was from this particular mosque that, in 1739, Nadir Shah had ordered the ruthless massacre of many inhabitants of Delhi. He also looted the famous Peacock Throne from the Diwan-e-Khas of the Red Fort, and took away the famous

Koh-i-Noor diamond. As we were walking under this mosque to reach the sweet shop of Ghante Wale, which is more than a century old, an ancient looking tramcar trundled past us towards the clock tower of Chandni Chowk.

Ghante Wale's shop of traditional sweets and savouries was a remarkable landmark of Chandni Chowk. Right from the early years of the nineteenth century, this shop was famous for its varieties of barfis, as well as its sohan halwa and dal moth. All these delicacies were prepared in pure ghee. The appearance of this shop was totally different from all the sweet shops of today. Here, every customer had to purchase sweets while standing on a footpath running next to the shop. Right before them, on a high platform or a counter, sat two salesmen of ample proportions dressed in spotless dhotis and kurtas with stiff black caps. They were surrounded on all sides with mounds of sweets.

The savouries were stocked in another wing of that shop. While all sweets were generally packed in reed baskets with covers, salted items were put into cones made out of old newspapers, and handed over to waiting customers with a flourish. The sun had set behind the clock tower, popularly called Ghanta Ghar, when we climbed into the tonga, carrying more than one reed basket as well as several paper cones. After that memorable afternoon at Lal Qila and evening in Chandni Chowk, we returned home riding through a park which at that time was officially called the Queen's Garden, but for the people of Delhi it was still the Company Bagh named after the East India Company.

We had a rather comic ending to our trip. As our tonga approached Mori Gate, the horse began to race towards its stable and not to our building on Nicholson Road. When the coachman cracked his whip, the horse kicked back with a resounding thud at the footboard of our tonga. At that point, my mother screamed at us for getting a tonga with such an ill-behaved horse.

And thus ended a memorable day in historic surroundings, in a city of kings and nobles; legends and tales. Even today, this visit seems etched in my mind. The details may fade away, but the experience lives on. The old city, seen from the eyes of a young boy, has changed dramatically. But, for me, the romance lingers; the aroma stays and the light never dims.

Part 2

Shades

Chapter 4

Aroma of Days Gone By

Food shop, Old Delhi, 1951

Aroma of Days Gone By

Those colourful shops of my days as a youngster were filled with paper kites. Kites of all the hues of a rainbow and in varied sizes. Every time I looked at them, it was almost as if the shades of my dreams were soaring before me

From the very beginning of the year 1943 we became used to the different way of life in Old Delhi. Our food habits, too, began to change rapidly with our surroundings. After settling down here my father began to pay considerable attention to his family, particularly with regard to the intake of food. It was also at this time of his life that he began to evolve his favourite theory of nutrition, which gave considerable preference to all meat and wheat products rather than the usual Bengali staple diet of rice, lentils and fish. Within a year of our coming to Delhi, the serving and eating of plain boiled rice had become almost taboo.

This strict edict regarding Bengali food had to be followed by not only everyone in our family, but also by the numerous relatives and friends who landed up at our place from Kolkata on every possible excuse. There was hardly a week at that time when our flat was not full. The situation was somewhat similar to what many Bengali expatriate families have to face today in London, New York and also probably in Silicon Valley.

The constant overcrowding of our flat, combined with the wartime shortage of daily food items such as wheat, sugar and bread, began to build a considerable amount of stress for my ever-accommodating mother. We two brothers, not yet in our teens, had to run frequent errands to the traditional bazaar that flourished along an old lane called Ganda Nalah, or to a distinctly British shopping mall at Kashmere Gate. Though this running of errands did create many difficulties in our educational routine and progress, we got a chance to see a different life pattern. Ganda Nalah, or 'Dirty Channel', was actually the name of a narrow street running behind our house. During the Mughal days it had been an open drain carrying effluents outside Mori Gate. Later this channel was filled and turned into a lane, which could only be reached from the level of Nicholson Road by going down a wide and public staircase. Those who had settled along that lane after the uprising of 1857 lived in a rather traditional manner. They were somewhat less prosperous than the people living around Nicholson Road or even Kashmere Gate.

This area was mainly a Muslim locality till September 1947 and had an interesting atmosphere of the old Mughal days. We had to go to this congested lane often, both for our daily needs such as meat and eggs, as well as to take a shortcut to some of the distinctly European-style shops and stores located around Kashmere Gate.

As we walked down the narrow lane of Ganda Nalah, most of the houses seen here were two-storeyed and had been built after the upheaval which the Old City and its inhabitants had to undergo in 1857-58. The origin of many occupants of these old houses could be traced back to the multitude of salatin, or royal pensioners who were driven out from the inner sanctum of the Red Fort by the new foreign rulers of Delhi. It is also said that many of these migrants to the Ganda Nalah and Mori Gate were royal ladies who were unfortunate enough to lose their men in the brutal reprisal by the British force. They had to eke out a living by doing tarkashi, or metal thread work on velvet and silk. Sometimes they also took part in running a small shop or a petty stall selling trinkets or items required for everyday use.

However, when we reached Delhi in 1942, life went on quite placidly around Ganda Nalah, with a variety of shops occupying the ground floor of nearly all the buildings and residential accommodation located on the upper floors. Many of the shops and houses located here had a characteristic old-world atmosphere. Many of those features reminded us about life in Delhi during the late Mughal days. All along the lane there were shops selling everything from vegetables and meat to perfumes and paper kites. Scattered among these shops was an eatery or two with kababs being cooked on a charcoal grill and roomali rotis, or kerchief-thin bread, tossed in the air before being cooked on an iron skittle shaped like a dome.

The ubiquitous paan and ittar shops seen around this part of the old lane have to be mentioned for their redolence. A curious mixture of exotic fragrances greeted our nostrils long before the actual perfume shop glittering with cut glass bottles and bright lights could be seen.

Then there were the beautiful stalls and sometimes fair-sized shops, too. Those colourful shops of my days as a youngster were filled with paper kites. Kites of all the hues of a rainbow and in varied sizes. Every time I looked at them, it was almost as if the shades of my dreams were soaring before me. I can never forget the mania that gripped the old city during the two monsoon months, when kite flying was at its peak. Stacks of colourful kites could be seen in the air along with glass-coated threads or manja. These threads had a cutting edge and were usually wound on a bamboo bobbin called charkhi.

During the rainy season of July and August, all the rooftops and open areas around Mori Gate were crowded with groups of people, both young and old, flying kites. Varieties of manja thread were used with great manoeuvring skills to cut the contestant's kite and, when one of them got cut, the traditional victory call of 'Voh Katta' rang out.

It is said that even the last Mughal Emperor of Delhi, Bahadur Shah Zafar, often indulged in this pastime of flying kites. Around the middle of the nineteenth century, Devendra Nath Tagore, father of the poet Rabindra Nath Tagore, while moving up the Yamuna, had seen the Emperor flying kites on a rooftop at the Red Fort. Apparently, before Bahadur Shah became Emperor, another prince lost his claim to the throne because of his habit of disappearing into the bazaar outside the palace to fly kites.

It was always interesting to watch life going on around this traditional, yet lively place. Here, all along Ganda Nalah, we could often see several goats and sheep tethered at many of the doorsteps either for milk, or for sacrifice on Eid. Sometimes two of those king-sized goats, while munching green leaves and with no sign of trouble, would suddenly rear up on their hind legs and butt one another fiercely. Among those tethered animals were also a variety of sheep called dumba, and these animals had fat-laden bulbous tails. Such tails were considered a great delicacy among traditional gourmets of north Indian cities, including Old Delhi.

Many of the verandahs and hanging balconies often had caged partridges kept in pairs. These fighting birds were used for betting which ran into large sums. Their owners, usually elderly men with flowing beards, would take them out to the gardens near Mori Gate every day. Aside from some fresh air, this was a way of keeping them fighting fit. Partridge fights could be seen in the early summer months or during the last days of spring. Another sport that kept rival groups busy was cock fighting, popular since the Mughal times.

After winding on further towards Kashmere Gate this narrow lane became rather derelict and crowded with old houses which, after a heavy shower or two, would collapse like a pack of cards. Our tailor Hakim Mian's house, for instance, just collapsed one morning, leaving him devastated. A year later, it was in this very lane that I saw another old house in ruins and this time three people died. In spite of such calamities, life went on in a traditional manner.

One fine morning in the autumn of 1943 we were surprised to see many men, women and even children assemble around a large tent called a shamiana, which had sprung up overnight outside Mori Gate. While many women covered in burqas were disappearing behind that well-screened enclosure, the men, dressed in their traditional costume of achkan and white caps, had begun to take their place on rugs spread out for their Eid prayers. For a few weeks before Eid, whenever my brother and I happened to go around Ganda Nalah, we would notice a definite change of air among the shops, big or small. All eating places would be closed for the day. Every evening there would be several stalls selling dry fruits that included plump, dark dates. As the sun went down, a loud boom coming from a firecracker was heard outside Mori Gate. Immediately all the shops, piled with edibles, began to do brisk business. A couple of hefty men loaded with skin bags began to clank their tinned metal bowls to offer cold water to the many passersby who had been fasting all through the day.

Another characteristic of this traditional locality, which we young boys found strange, was almost the total absence of women or girls above the age of four or five. All the women were secluded in the well-screened first floors of their residential rooms and, whenever they needed to come out for some business or pleasure, they would be covered in their burqas, usually black or white and sometimes green. But that did not prevent them from being heard above the usual audible level of that lane. Often peals of high-pitched giggles and some laughter came through those opaque coverings or, at times, from those first-floor verandahs that were hidden with reed screens called chiks.

A lane in Mori Gate, 1952

On some rare evenings, we could also hear the distant strains of ghazals or thumri recitals. But sadly, soon after August 15, 1947, the old-world charm of Ganda Nalah vanished almost overnight from our locality. Many of the families who had been living there for long were destined to lose their ancestral homes. When we walked further towards the locality called Kashmere Gate, the name, as well as the general character of this maze of old lanes, changed rather abruptly before ending near the colonial shopping complex. While one branch of the lane joined a wide road called Hamilton Road, running along the railway line, the other branch, after some twists and turns, became Chhabi Gunj, before ending near the ornate iron gate of the old Hindu College. Even in that narrow stretch there was more than one big bungalow and the most imposing one belonged to a rich banker called Lala Sultan Singh.

This spacious building, built like a castle, stood on a large garden complete with a few peacocks and a pet deer or two. We heard those peacocks often, but seldom saw any deer. Only once we managed to see a small barking deer after it had escaped from that well-guarded house and was being chased furiously by three or four guards in khaki uniforms. When the iron gates of the bungalow swung open we would see vintage cars such as a Lancia Lamda or a huge eight-cylinder Buick roll into that estate.

The other interesting bungalow on the lane happened to be the ancestral home of my physics teacher, Professor DS Mathur. After joining Hindu College, whenever I visited him to get a tough physics problem solved, I could not help but wonder at many of the English bay-windows as well as arched doorways of that old residence built after the upheaval of 1857.

A short distance from these two houses, the narrow lane of Chhabigunj opened out to the smart shopping area of Kashmere Gate. Here the presence of St. James' Church and a triangular park, where military bands played often on Sundays, further heightened the colonial ambience of that open square and the shopping complex.

St. James' Church, was built in Palladian style, in the early nineteenth century as the fulfilment of a vow taken by Colonel James Skinner, while lying wounded at a battlefield near Delhi. Right in front of this church, and across the wide road, was the main shopping area of Kashmere Gate. Here, almost all shops had English names and catered mainly to the British as well as many Anglo-Indian families living in Civil Lines.

We were sent to those shops often in search of foodstuff ranging from English marmalade and biscuits to many delicacies such as smoked ham and cheddar cheese. Spencer's sold tinned provisions and wines while Keventer's was generally known for its pasteurised milk and other dairy products, such as butter and soft cream cheese. While Kemp & Co was one of the main chemist shops, Bata's shoe shop was always flourishing and is still going strong. As for restaurants and bars, Carlton Café had been doing well and during the war years we would see many British army personnel loitering around this restaurant with their girl friends.

This particular shopping mall at Kashmere Gate flourished for more than twenty years and resembled the famous shopping mall of Shimla, the summer capital of British India. At both places a common feature in all the buildings were the gabled tin roofs. That style of architecture made Sir Edwin Lutyens, the chief designer of New Delhi, rather angry and he came out with a caustic remark that even if monkeys had created that chaotic style of architecture they deserved to be shot.

Apart from being a smart shopping centre and evening promenade meant for the 'Sahib log' living in Delhi's Civil Lines, this particular area of Kashmere Gate had the distinction of being home to some of the finest academic institutions in Old Delhi. In the early fifties, I had the good fortune of attending a few practical classes in science at a unique school building which, in Mughal times, had been the library and home of Prince Dara Shukoh, Emperor Shah Jahan's favourite son. Just off Lothian Road, the entire palace had been rebuilt after Lord Lake captured Delhi in 1803 and it became the first British Residency. Some of the notable British Residents such as General Ochterlony and Sir Charles Metcalfe stayed in the same building and later, when the Residency was shifted, this historical bungalow became Delhi's first college before being turned into a high school run by Delhi Polytechnic.

The other historic building at Kashmere Gate was once the residence of Colonel James Skinner and his family. That sprawling old bungalow was the campus of my college, Hindu College, till 1953, and also a typical example of early British residences in Delhi. It was once a two-storeyed bungalow with deep verandahs and thick columns running on all sides. The main building had large halls as living rooms, which later became lecture theatres of our college. Some of the outhouses were converted into science laboratories.

There was also an annex shaped like an open rotunda which functioned as the assembly hall of our college. It was the main venue for many of our functions. At the same place we often heard leading political leaders such as Lok Nayak Jai Prakash Narayan and the famous scientist, Dr Homi Bhabha. While Dr Bhabha, dressed in an impeccable suit, elaborated about the exciting world of atomic energy, Jai Prakash Narayan wore the red cap of a socialist leader and criticised some of the leading industrialists of Delhi who were supporting our college to the hilt.

While the main bungalow was demolished to make way for a modern municipal building, the old rotunda hall still survives, though boarded

Lane in Old Delhi, 1952

up with crude wooden planks. Any reference to my college takes me back to an incident that took place on a hot and sultry afternoon of July 1952. The lunch bell had just rung, and I was on the look-out for our cook Nehaluji, an elderly lady, who was always dressed in a spotless white sari. For a paltry sum of five rupees extra on her monthly salary, she brought my lunch to college on all afternoons till the end of 1952.

Under the shade of an old neem tree, which grew at a little distance from the ancient building, she would spread the meal neatly on a rug complete with a plate and all the necessary forks and spoons. For this highly unusual practice, I had to undergo a fair amount of ragging from my fellow students.

On that particular day, as I sat down to eat, Nehaluji handed me a small slip of paper from my mother and added in a solemn tone that I must read it first. Though hungry, I had no other choice but to read that note, and what I did read was important enough to nearly make me forget all about lunch and rush home.

My first photo feature on historic monuments of Delhi had been accepted and would soon be published. Even now, fifty years later, I recall how thrilled I was with this news. That year in 1952, I was in the very first year of my college, and my father, once again, was about to lose his job at the All India Radio, mainly for writing his well-known autobiography.

I, as the eldest son, had to do something to help the family and I had to continue with my college studies. I tried to combine my skill with a camera with my familiarity with the city of Delhi and put it to good use. My first attempt towards this purpose had obviously clicked, and the feature 'Charming Delhi Views' was published on August 17 of that year. Two out of the six pictures published in that feature were taken with the good old box camera which had come to Delhi with us in 1942.

The historic city of Delhi, along with that humble little camera, had literally pushed me into an exciting career of photojournalism and mass media for more than half a century.

Chapter 5

Growing with the Flow

Pir Ghaib, 2003

Growing with the Flow

Watching birds all along the wild sand banks of the Yamuna and among the jungles of the Northern Ridge became an exciting and favourite pastime

If there was any area, which till the late forties of the last century could be described as a distinct British settlement in Delhi, it was definitely Civil Lines. Whenever we happened to come out of the confines of the old city outside Kashmere Gate, or for that matter even Mori Gate, the cityscape changed completely from an old North Indian city to a spacious urban area, which was totally different in ambience and colour.

Though the two main roads running through Civil Lines had typical Indian names such as Alipur and Rajpur Road, many other roads had distinct English names such as Flagstaff Road, Underhill Road as well as Metcalfe Road, named after the British Resident Sir Thomas Metcalfe. His palatial house called Metcalfe House still stands near the Yamuna. Many of the buildings such as Ludlow Castle, Maiden's Hotel or the Exchange Store, were very English in their names and appearances.

Here, in Civil Lines, most of the residential houses were very different from those inside the old city and almost all the buildings took the form of spacious single-storeyed bungalows with well laid-out gardens. Many of the nameplates displayed on the gates of these bungalows had obvious English names as well as titles. The nameplates often competed with ubiquitous 'Beware of Dog' signs in no uncertain terms.

On many a bright winter day, we would see an English family sipping beer or tea in their flowering garden, with a couple of spaniels or retrievers jumping around them, playing with a tennis ball.

This locality with English characteristics had come up rapidly after the upheaval of 1857. Civil Lines here had well-defined boundaries, with the Ridge rising towards the west, and the Yamuna flowing along the east. The old city wall between Kashmere Gate and Mori Gate marked the southern limit of this British area of Old Delhi. For more than two decades after Delhi was declared the capital city, Civil Lines functioned as the centre for British India, before it was finally shifted to New Delhi in 1932.

Ten years later, when we first came to Delhi, Civil Lines had retained a good deal of its colonial atmosphere. This was because many of the English officials and professionals such as architects, lawyers and even horticulturists continued to live in this spacious and quiet area. The main territory of Delhi province was under the control of an English Chief Commissioner, who could often be seen around his house and garden on Ludlow Castle Road.

Among professionals, the sight of the veteran British architect, Sir Walter George, driving about in an ancient Rolls Royce, with a pipe dangling from his lips, and also the horticulturist, Percy Lancaster, pottering about in the garden full of hollyhocks, reminded me that this particular colony in Delhi was still rather English, reminscient of books written by Rudyard Kipling or PG Wodehouse. This distinct influence of British imperial power was further enhanced by the presence of public buildings such as the Old Secretariat and the old Viceregal Lodge, which had already become part of the campus of Delhi University.

From the front verandah of our flat, which overlooked Civil Lines, the view was of a solid green landscape and hardly that of a capital city. Only some of the landmarks such as the Flagstaff Tower, the twin towers of the Old Secretariat, along with the top-floor colonnade of Maiden's Hotel, all visible over a dense foliage of trees, gave the impression that we were looking at an old Imperial city. There were also many playgrounds and lawns just outside the walled city. These, along with gardens, Nicholson Park and Qudsia Bagh, were maintained by the British authorities.

Almost every day we would see a tall Englishman, the Deputy Commissioner of Delhi, strolling in and around Civil Lines with a shooting stick. He kept a strict vigil on everything. At that time we young boys played in these parks and fields. But soon after World War II ended, we began to explore deep into Civil Lines as well as take frequent long walks along the banks of the Yamuna and the thickly-wooded slopes of the northern Ridge.

The reasons behind this change in our regular outdoor activities were divergent, if not rather amusing. The first, and probably the most important of these factors which brought about this change, was the arrival of our dog Rex, a large golden retriever, from the kennel of the Maharaja of Jind. The second reason happened to be the addition of Dr Salim Ali's book on Indian birds to my father's already diverse library. That book, combined with a pair of old binoculars gifted by an English colonel returning to England, created a good deal of interest as well as excitement in our family. Watching birds all along the wild sand banks of the Yamuna and among the jungles of the Ridge became a favourite pastime.

The third and final factor responsible for this change, though remote and somewhat far-fetched, could be attributed to the unexpected defeat of Prime Minister Winston Churchill and his Conservative Party in England at the election of July 1945. That rejection of Churchill by the British people upset my father a great deal. He immediately began to write about English politics and, for relaxation, would go for long walks to watch birds with us and Rex.

Since we lived in a flat and Rex had to be taken out for his morning ablutions and exercise early, we usually began our trips to the river not later than six every morning. After coming out of Mori Gate, we had to walk along with a crowd of pious Hindu men and women, all heading for the holy river flowing quietly beyond Qudsia Bagh. Most of these men and women usually wore their traditional costumes of a dhoti or a sari and carried small baskets of flowers in their hands. They often chanted 'Hari Om Hari' and 'Jai Sita Ram' as they walked at a brisk pace towards the Yamuna.

On certain festive days such as Janmashtami or Kartik Purnima, the number of people in these crowds easily went up to more than a thousand. Quite a few of them came not only from Mori Gate and Kashmere Gate, but also from the deep interiors of the old city and localities such as Bazaar Sita Ram or Khari Baoli and from a lane called Katra Neel.

After crossing the playgrounds and lawns outside Mori Gate we had to go past an old cemetery where Brigadier General John Nicholson lay buried since1857. The place was full of dark and sombre clusters of trees and many horned owls lived here, hooting long after the sun had risen well above the horizon.

On the other side of the road was a well-laid park with tall palm trees and the statue of General Nicholson.

Qudsia Bagh, located across Alipur Road, was a large garden that was once the pleasure garden of a Mughal queen called Qudsia Begum. Originally from the world of entertainment, she became the wife of Emperor Muhammed Shah. She wielded considerable power and influence in the Mughal court of the late eighteenth century. This garden was a pleasure resort till the reign of Bahadur Shah Zafar. This large and historical garden has now been considerably attenuated by the Interstate Bus Terminal, concrete flyovers and the elevated Metro Rail. The entire area, with many tennis lawns and even a Freemason's lodge, was a real beauty spot of our young days.

After entering Qudsia Garden we had to walk past a ruined gate and an old mosque before we could reach the Yamuna, where ghats and ashrams lined the bank. Here, all along the river which glistened under the morning sun, there would always be a crowd, bathing and worshipping. The men usually chanted 'Jai Shiv Shankar' after having a dip, while women poured milk or water over the Shiva lingam present in many of those ghats. (The entire ambience of religious sight and sound was like the miniature version of a grand audiovisual phenomenon seen every day at the ghats of Varanasi.)

From those ghats we could see the red walls of the Red Fort, along with the steel girders of the railway bridge. Till the middle sixties this was the only bridge that connected Delhi with Uttar Pradesh. On this bridge we would often see steam engines blowing dark smoke trails. Sometimes, when we went to the river in the evening, we could see funeral pyres with leaping flames and curling smoke rising over Nigambodh Ghat, an old cremation ground.

The various spectacles of fire, ancient and modern, along the river remind me of an impressive yagna ceremony that took place on the eastern bank of the Yamuna in the mid-forties. There, a huge worshipping hall, along with numerous pilgrims' huts, was set up with bamboo poles and reed matting. Improvised wooden and bamboo bridges were also built. Country boats ferried devotees who had flocked to attend that ceremony. Once there, everyone could hear the sonorous chanting of Vedic mantras and witness the constant offerings of ghee and incense into the sacred fire, which went on throughout the day.

A strange phenomenon, which could be observed around this place of worship, was that no one objected to our non-pious appearances and the presence of a huge dog waiting patiently outside the worshipping hall. Sadly enough, a few days before all rituals and ceremonies could end, the sacred fire went out of control, and within minutes the entire pavilion and the surrounding structures were reduced to heaps of smouldering ash.

In our young days at the height of summer we often tried to learn swimming in the Yamuna, and though impossible to believe today, the water was rather deep and the current, too, was swift. One day, while paddling in a stretch of chest-deep water, I got dragged into a deep whirlpool. But Rex, along with our cousin Sanat, who was an expert swimmer, literally pulled me out of that pool of water into a shallow spot near a ghat.

A few years later, when another cousin Chinmoy arrived in Delhi, we tried to resume our swimming lessons. One day, all of a sudden, we came across a danger, which in a river so near Delhi, could hardly be imagined. All regular bathing ghats were rather crowded on that particular day, and to avoid that crowding we went to a boat club jetty near Metcalfe House. There the river was rather shallow and also quiet. But as we did a good deal of splashing and shouting after getting into the river, a man rushed out of a boat club hut and ordered us to come out of the water immediately. As it happened, a large crocodile had been spotted the previous evening near a boat, and someone getting into that particular boat had a narrow escape from being attacked. So, instead of having a hungry crocodile as a fellow swimmer, we decided to move back once again to a crowded ghat without any protest. Our luck at that time, however, was totally against us, and my younger brother Kirti came down with a bad attack of typhoid.

Crocodiles, infected water and also the sighting of various kinds of snakes did nothing to curb our enthusiasm for the river and its wild and secluded banks. Though the British Resident, Sir Thomas Metcalfe, had built his palatial house right on the river bank, many other areas, particularly towards the east, had little human habitation and appeared to be rather wild.

The whole countryside beyond the river was a bird watcher's paradise. We could often spot varieties of cranes, spoonbills and snipes. Sometimes even flamingoes came down there, and waded about in stretches of shallow water after dipping their beaks. Many a lapwing couple could be seen all over those sand banks, and whenever we happened to chance upon their nests, one of the two birds would flutter

Sir Walter George, 1957

and try to distract us with its characteristic "did-he-do-it" call. At the same swampy ground we would sometimes spot an elusive jacana with a curved black-feathered tail. A rare sighting of that bird prancing around in a water pool always created a flurry of excitement.

On a cold winter morning of those colonial days we happened to see the grand spectacle of an English foxhunt.

By sheer chance that Sunday morning we had stopped at a high embankment near Metcalfe House. There, on the wild scrubland across the river, a group of English horsemen, dressed in short coats and tight breeches, were galloping away with their packs of fox hounds in the lead.

The scruffy old jackal seemed to have completely eluded the trail that morning, and a horn sounded to end that day's hunt.

Hunting on the banks of the Yamuna was not a pastime for English rulers alone. Getting back to the middle of the 19th century, it is on record that Emperor Bahadur Shah Zafar went hunting on these banks often. Once the hunt was over, the Emperor distributed the venison among all his followers as a prized bounty.

There is also a legend in the Bhagavat Purana that in the ancient age of Mahabharata, Lord Krishna, along with his disciple and friend Arjuna, did many a mrigaya or shikar on the banks of the Yamuna, near Indraprastha. Once, the legendary kings chanced upon an ashram while washing in the river. That ashram belonged to an ascetic princess called Kalindi because of her dark complexion. With that age-old story that spot on the Yamuna came to be known as Kalindi Kunj.

Moving on from the river to the Civil Line's Ridge, we made it a point to visit that hilly terrain usually with the oncoming of the rainy season. In Delhi, those days, the summer curtain of dust and the winter mist vanished like magic. All trees and the old buildings on the Ridge, as well as Pir Ghaib and Chauburji Masjid, began to resemble a painting by Constable rather than a Turner. The northern stretch of Delhi's Ridge stretched from Sabzi Mandi, one of the oldest suburbs of the city, to Mall Road, near the university. Actually it began to roll down after the Flagstaff Tower and ended at a miniature pass with an old bazaar, the area jokingly called Delhi's Khyber Pass by British soldiers. The entire stretch of this rocky hill, along Rajpur Road, had a jungle of hardy babul or the Indian acacia tree.

In addition, many of the large flowering trees such as the flame of the forest, Indian silk cotton and laburnums, lent a touch of varied colours to the dense green vegetation of the northern Ridge. Apart from this unusual jungle with many flowering trees, what made the Ridge interesting was the presence of more than one historical site.

Our favourite spot to watch the landscape around Civil Lines was a pyramid-shaped old ruin called Pir Ghaib. This gaunt stone building was also known as Khushk-i-Shikar, or a hunting lodge. Built probably by Feroz Shah Tughlaq in the fourteenth century, many historians were of the view that this unique structure functioned originally as an observatory. Whatever it was, for us it was one of the most interesting observation points which could be found around the Ridge. Once we managed to get onto the high platform above Pir Ghaib the view from that vantage point was really breathtaking. Even without our binoculars we could spot all the landmarks of Civil Lines clearly. There was also a wonderful view of the Yamuna as well as that of the old city from the top of this unique Tughlaq ruin.

Among many of the other well-known landmarks that could be seen from Pir Ghaib, the Ludlow Castle with its turreted roof happened to be the nearest to our vantage point. A little further towards the east was the grand façade of the Maiden's Hotel, one of the oldest European hotels of Delhi. It exists even today. Looking further north one could also see the rebuilt Metcalfe House and the twin towers of the Old Secretariat building. Those towers which once ruled India from Civil Lines seemed to silently proclaim the Imperial age.

From the Ridge we could clearly make out the tall black chimney of the waterworks which was then the main supplier of potable water to the city, including New Delhi. Way back in the winter months of 1955, the effluent from the Najafgarh canal got sucked into this water supply and a good number of people, including my mother, came down with a serious attack of jaundice. The outbreak of this epidemic, along with the pollution of the Yamuna water, took such a serious turn that Pandit Nehru had to face many questions in Parliament. Two of our other favourite observation points along the Ridge were the Tughlaq building, Chauburji Masjid, or the four-domed mosque, and the Flagstaff Tower built by the British.

While Chauburji Masjid had a limited view because of many large trees around it, Flagstaff Tower was free from such obstacles and presented a splendid view of the western side of the Ridge. The old Viceregal Lodge, which had become Delhi University, was situated right at the foot of the Ridge. After climbing up Flagstaff Tower, we could see the old cantonment area dotted with ruined pillboxes and abandoned ammunition magazines. The lone brick tower of St. Stephen's College was the only exception in that rugged landscape beyond the Ridge.

While walking towards Hindu Rao House, next to Pir Ghaib, we often took the equestrian track, which, till then, was a unique British feature found on Delhi's Ridge. This earthen path, strewn with sawdust, wound through a densely-wooded area of lantana bush. We could often spot animals such as jackals, foxes and brown hares particularly at dusk. One late evening, as we were returning from the Ridge,

Rex, who had been trotting in front, refused to move and began to growl fiercely while staring at a dark lantana bush. Though Rex had been trained for hunting he was usually a gentle dog and would not have bothered to growl for nothing. After a short spell of silence we heard some heavy animals rushing away before they could actually be seen. A few days later we came to know from a local gardener that a couple of lakkad baggas or striped hyenas had strayed into that area of the Ridge because of the heavy flooding of the Yamuna beds.

This encounter happened right under an old house called the Hindu Rao House which, though a hospital now, was the residence of British Commissioner, William Fraser. One night, while riding back from a dinner party at Daryagunj, Fraser was shot by an assassin and he died just before entering his house. That bungalow was later bought by a Maratha chief called Hindu Rao and later converted into a well-known hospital.

Near this lonely spot was a large slab of rock which formed a natural bird table for many wild birds. They ranged from peacocks to flocks of chattering babblers and blossom-headed parakeets. Every morning some of the Jain traders from Sabzi Mandi came up to this particular stone and scattered coarse grains such as millets and grams for the birds. It was here that I once watched a dancing peacock with its tail spread like an upright fan while many peahens were busy feeding and did not even spare a single glance at the strutting male bird. At times we could spot more than thirty species of birds all over the Ridge. However, one winter morning when we spotted a flock of scarlet minivet in a clump of trees, that sighting became very special indeed.

Apart from dozens of noisy babblers, what added to the natural decibel level at this spot were the common parrots with red rings circling their necks and crimson beaks. This particular species was always to be found at this feeding rock and at the least provocation from human beings these birds fluttered up like an emerald whirlwind, and all trees nearby became dotted with shrieking red-beaked parakeets.

Once, the famous Bengali author of *Pather Panchali*, the late Bibhuti Bhushan Banerjee, came to visit us in Delhi. Owing to his love of nature we took him for a walk through the Ridge as well as to the natural bird table. Our visitor was rather pleased to find a large flock of parrots pecking grams on that stone. After spotting us there the entire flock of parrots suddenly rose up in a flutter of bright green hues. We had the greatest difficulty in persuading this nature-loving author to return home for dinner, scheduled exactly at seven.

We began to notice many changes in the European character of Civil Lines soon after World War II ended. As chance would have it, I had a first hand experience to observe this change at a place no other than Maiden's Hotel. For a few months in early 1946, an English war widow who had been a colleague of my father, stayed in that hotel and in her spare time gave us lessons in reciting English poetry. From her room high up at Maiden's we could not only see the entire Civil Lines but also the preparations for World War II Victory Day celebrations. For nearly a week in March 1946, flags were flying all over Delhi and many buildings of Civil Lines were also flood-lit. Then in the morning that day my father suddenly returned home, somewhat shaken, and told us that while walking to the Broadcasting House in New Delhi a large group of demonstrators asked him to take off his hat and tie. So, he returned home quietly and asked us not to go to the parade ground near Red Fort. However, in the evening we managed to go for a walk with Rex up Alipore Road and found no trace of any celebration in Civil Lines. Only a few armoured cars were roaring about in the streets with British army personnel looking quite grim. Within a matter of weeks our kind teacher, Mrs Evelyn Wood, moved away from the Maiden's. She, along with many of her fellow countrymen, left Delhi's Civil Lines for good.

Shades of life during the British times play on my memory. Those were the days of my boyhood when exciting discoveries along the Yamuna and on the Ridge filled our lives with excitement and promise.

Chapter 6

Winds of Change

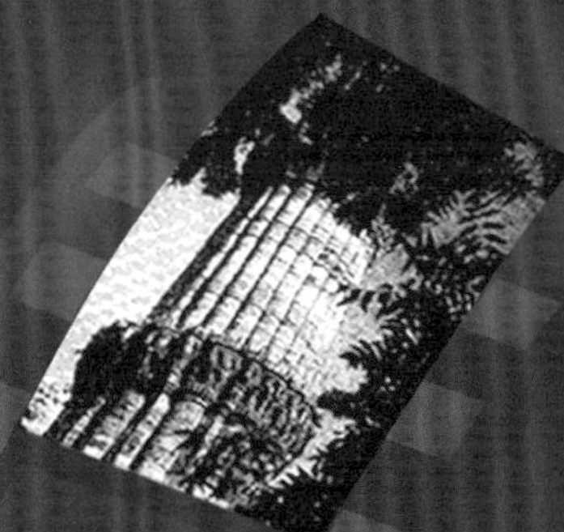

All India Radio, Broadcasting House, 1953

Winds of Change

Having mastered the skill to move around with ease on my bicycle, exploring all areas of Delhi, both the old and the new, became almost a craze for me, along with a passion for photography

Towards the beginning of the summer of 1947, it became quite clear to us living in Delhi that the end of British rule in India was an immediate reality and no longer a distant dream. Though the Cabinet Mission of 1946 sent by Prime Minister Clement Atlee had to return without tangible success, an interim government under the leadership of Pandit Jawaharlal Nehru was already in position in New Delhi. This change at the top level of the Government resulted in an outflow of British officers working at various levels in Delhi as well as all over India. At that time I had just completed fourteen and, like a young beaver on a prowl, was eager to rush around this city.

At this awkward age, when one is neither a boy nor an adult, and with the eagerness to explore something new, I learnt to ride a bicycle with certain zeal and proficiency. Having mastered the skill to move around with ease on my bicycle, exploring all areas of Delhi, both the old and the new, became almost a craze for me, along with a passion for photography.

Shops all over Delhi were full of imported goodies such as motorcars, radios and edibles such as Huntley & Palmer's biscuits, Chiver's jams and many varieties of strong-smelling cheese. But, for me, the best of all those imported items happened to be photographic films, which once again were freely available. Long queues of men and women, often seen at photo shops, had disappeared for good. Whenever an amount of rupees five, usually received as a gift from a relative, could be managed I would buy a roll of film for a rupee-and-a-half.

Then, setting aside two rupees and eight annas for processing, I would hire a cycle to move around in Delhi.

Connaught Place, 1953

While my photographic activities were restricted at that time to nothing further than the Yamuna or the Ridge, my readiness to run errands on a bicycle took me often to Connaught Place as well as to Broadcasting House for delivering some of my father's scripts.

Connaught Place, designed by the architect RT Russell, was an impressive shopping arcade built for the elite of New Delhi with colonial inclinations and taste. Even the four cinema houses with their distinctive English names of Odeon, Plaza, Regal and Rivoli served as important landmarks around that impressive shopping arcade. Till the late fifties, those cinema houses of New Delhi usually showed English films from Hollywood. I might add here that for us youngsters most of those cinema houses were out of bounds. We did manage to see three films till 1947 and they were more or less documentaries such as *Desert Victory*, *Victory Through Air Power* and Disney's *Fantasia*, based on European classical music.

I was sent often to that shopping area mainly for three things required for entertaining my father's colleagues and friends. These were the wonderful cakes and pastries from the Swiss pastry shop of Wenger's; smoked ham as well as strong-smelling cheese such as Gorgonzola, which my father loved to inflict upon his Indian guests with glee, along with some vintage wine. At times I had also to search for some elusive flowers such as narcissus and choose strawberries from hawkers, who were seen around Connaught Place for barely a week.

My father's other favourite shops included the exclusive Army and Navy Store at Regal Building. It sold everything from vintage champagne to Hornby model trains. Phelps and Ranken were his tailors and drapers at that time. All our china articles such as a Mason dinner service along with Paragon coffee cups were the specialties of a shop at Queen's Way called Sutherland. Curiously enough, Manton, at Scindia House, mainly known for selling guns and fishing rods, also sold glittering cut glass vases and colourful Toby jugs. A bookshop next door, though owned by a Sindhi family, had the classical English name of Oxford Book Store.

All establishments around Connaught Place had signboards in quite a low key and there were no conspicuous hoardings or neon signs visible, except at the four cinema houses. On a bright day hundreds of columns gleaming white all around that shopping arcade lent an impressive display of splendour to Delhi's unique Connaught Place.

Apart from Connaught Place, the other landmark I got to visit quite often was the Broadcasting House on Parliament Street. Since my father appeared to be rather upset with many of the political happenings in India as well as in the UK, he began to write some forthright articles for English newspapers and magazines. He would often send me to the All India Radio with a home-written script, and while on such missions I began to observe many interesting aspects of New Delhi towards the end of the British rule.

My options for covering the distance of about four-odd miles from our house to Broadcasting House by bus was extremely tedious and, depending on the route chosen, rather expensive. There were only two services running from Kashmere Gate to the Central Secretariat of New Delhi at that time. The first of them, route number two, happened to be the oldest in Delhi and was at first run by a company called GNIT or Gwalior and North Indian Transport.

All the buses were notoriously irregular as well as extremely slow-moving. Many vehicles on this route were old and ramshackled and broke down frequently in the crowded locality around Lahore Gate.

Pullman Service on route number nine had good buses, painted cream colour, but as the fare was steep, eight annas each way, this service catered mainly to senior government officers commuting from Old Delhi. So, my choice to reach New Delhi was rather limited and I had to either hire a boy's cycle, or if the weather was right, just walk the whole distance to Connaught Place or Broadcasting House.

The route to New Delhi I preferred to take while cycling or walking was to go past Tis Hazari Maidan and the rugged stone building of St. Stephen's Hospital, one of the oldest women's hospitals, where my mother, an aunt, and, many years later, my wife received urgent medical attention. Then, after crossing a railway bridge called Pul Mithai, or sweetseller's bridge, I had to take the Qutb Road right up to the nondescript New Delhi station and the rather dingy Pahargunj. After that point the same road came to be called Chelmsford Road till the outer circle of Connaught Place. Once there, the roads were almost empty, and with no restrictions on turning right one could easily go past the Regal Cinema and Lloyds Bank, to Parliament Street.

Those days Parliament Street was really a wonderful tree-lined avenue with no multi-storeyed buildings around. Only the Parliament House appeared at the end of a carefully planned vista. On regular office days two cycle tracks running on both sides of this road used to swarm with thousands of cyclists pedalling their way to the Secretariat in the morning. Almost everyone had a tiffin carrier hanging from the handlebar of his cycle. In those years eating food other than what was home-made was in more ways than one considered fit only for the English. Or for those Indians who usually came from the highly anglicised class such as ICS officers.

The motor traffic on that important street of New Delhi was negligible at all hours and one could walk across without any concern. The public buses that used to run appeared only after a long interval and, at times, none could be seen for more than an hour. As for the cars, they were mostly little Austin or Morris, with a sprinkling of large American cars such as Ford V-8 and Oldsmobile. Besides those ubiquitous common vehicles, luxury cars such as Bentley, Hawkers Siddley, Humber and also a few Rolls Royces could be seen, with the red number plates from the Indian princely states.

Broadcasting House was one of those rare government buildings, at that time, which

Naya Bazaar, 1953

required a pass to enter its impressive portals. But usually I got away without much trouble, because most of the regular guards knew me as Chhota, or Junior Chaudhuri Sahib. They also knew that I was heading towards Charles Barnes' room, the Director of the News Services Division of the All India Radio. Then, one morning we heard that Charles Barnes was returning home to England and within a few weeks I got a rare chance to ride a bullock cart all through New Delhi to his official bungalow on Safdarjung Road.

The reason for my riding such an animal-powered old conveyance through many roads and streets of New Delhi had become necessary because Father decided to acquire a Regency dining table and matching chairs along with other pieces of furniture from his outgoing chief. So, one early summer morning long before sunrise, I set off alone for the very limit of Lutyens' Delhi. I rode a bullock cart with four steel-rimmed wheels, a second one following our trail. Since the cart drivers as well as their bullocks plied often at the grain mart of Naya Bazaar on Burn Bastion Road they made a beeline for that area first before passing through the red-light area of Delhi called GB or Garstin Bastion Road.

After reaching the historic red building of Delhi College and also Ghazi-ud-din's Tomb situated outside Ajmere Gate, my fellow travellers, both human and animal, decided to have water from a charitable piao, or a free water stall. While we relaxed for a while outside that Mughal-period building, a call for the morning prayer came from a mosque right inside the college. As I tried to relax for a few minutes while looking at the early morning sky, flocks of pigeons could be seen flying in endless circles against that eastern sky over Turkman Gate.

After circling Connaught Circus anti-clockwise, which would not have been possible today, we trundled along Parliament Street and passed the brick clock tower and the main building of the New Delhi Town Hall. In the first few years after coming to Delhi we used to visit this town hall to see art exhibitions from Bengal. Two artists whose work I remember were Jamini Roy and Professor Ramen Chakravarty. But by early 1947 the venue of Delhi's art exhibitions had already shifted to the AIFACS gallery housed in a temporary wartime church on Parliament Street.

Next, we had to turn left into a narrow road called Old Mill Road. Proceeding along Parliament Street further would have landed our primitive transport in trouble because all around Parliament House, and the two Central Secretariat blocks, 'No Bullock Carts' signs were prominently displayed and observed with considerable vigour.

Old Mill Road had that curious name on account of a stone crusher mill operating at the site of Chemsford Club of New Delhi, which my bullock cart passed before reaching King's Way or Rajpath of today.

As my bullock cart passed the club, which was second only to the exclusive Gymkhana Club, I remembered that my father had created quite a sensation at a farewell party by wearing a white tie and a formal tailcoat, while all his English superiors, including Bozman, the Information and Broadcasting Secretary, attended the party in tuxedos.

After crossing the Central Vista at a fast pace to avoid meeting any of the many contingents of mounted police, who were frequently seen patrolling around Imperial Delhi, my cart drivers decided to take the winding route of Sunehri Bagh and Tughlaq Road to reach Charles Barnes' house near Safdarjung's Tomb. It was around half-past nine when I finally managed to reach my destination at the edge of Lutyens' Delhi. Charles Barnes and his personal assistant, Mrs Khinsaw, who later became his second wife, were at their chhota hazri table set up on the lush green lawn of a British bungalow. I must have appeared like a human scarecrow after my tough journey. I was covered from head to foot with tawny Delhi dust. But my father's English chief and his Burmese companion were rather kind and asked me to join them at the table for a wonderful English breakfast.

After loading all the items of furniture, including that ornate dining table, the two bullock carts set off at a brisk pace towards Old Delhi. However, the sun was quite hot by that time and I had to sit under the large dining table to keep myself cool. Even then, it was good to travel under the shade provided by the green trees that were planted all over New Delhi. More than a decade later at a seminar arranged in New Delhi I learnt from Sir Walter George, a British architect settled in Delhi, how neem trees were chosen for Aurangzeb Road, arjuna for Queen's Way and jamun for Ashoka. As chance would have it, I had to pass through those very roads on my return journey to Mori Gate. Sir Walter also described in that seminar in 1957 that the original topography around the entire area of New Delhi closely resembled the rocky and rugged look of the ruin-scattered Mehrauli.

As those two furniture-laden carts rattled along Queen's Way, my cart drivers were rather hesitant to pass through Connaught Circus in broad daylight. They decided to turn into the jamun-clad avenue of Ashoka Road where a little coppersmith bird had gone amuck with its spring song. Soon we hit the War Memorial Arch, now called India Gate, and minutes later saw the statue of King George V gazing solemnly towards the Viceroy's House where Lord Louis Mountbatten had just taken over as the last Viceroy of British India.

After the arrival of his newly-acquired furniture, my father began to entertain his colleagues and other friends. Among them, an elderly gentleman, Sayyid Mehmud Rizvi, soon became quite close to our family. Since Rizvi Sahib had unfortunately lost his wife long before he came to Delhi, his household was looked after by

Chaudhuri family at Mori Gate, 1948

his teenaged daughter Nargis and a married niece, Zubeida, and her husband, whom we called Mutahir Bhai. When Hindu-Muslim problems were erupting in an ugly manner all over the country, our families had become very good friends after a week-long holiday at the ancestral home of the Rizvi family at Rui Mandi in Agra City.

In New Delhi, Rizvi Sahib had been staying in a government colony called Aram Bagh, which was located close to the area known as Pahargunj, and everyone from our family was always welcome at his house. A short distance from this row of government houses, on Jhandewalan ridge, there was a Tughlaq ruin like Pir Ghaib called Bholi Bhatiari. But, according to Rizvi Sahib, who happened to be an Urdu scholar as well as a poet, the correct name of that historic ruin should have been Bu-Ali-Bakhtiari. Since I did have a great fascination for every historic building of Delhi, as well as for the rich pasanda kabab which Zubeida Baji always served with some crisp bakarkhani roti, I would walk or cycle down to Aram Bagh at every possible opportunity.

From our house on Nicholson Road, I usually took the route that went through localities with rather exotic names such as Barah Tooti, Pahari Dhiraj and Kadam Sharif. At the very end I had to pass through Ahta Kedara and Chuna Mandi before reaching Rizvi Sahib's house near Pahargunj. Most of the places I went through had distinct mohullas with predominantly Hindu or Muslim communities. Even at that young age of fourteen, what I could observe and also hear in those areas made me feel quite uneasy and apprehensive.

In all Hindu localities, where there was a park or an open space, young men in khaki shorts and white shirts did varied military exercises. Soon after their physical training these young men would salute a saffron flag. They would then be served a glass of milk or lassi made with churned yogurt.

In Muslim areas I noticed that many of these physical exercises took place usually in the evening. At first they had the form of a game of hockey and later those hockey sticks were turned into mock weapons for all types of combat training. Then came a few seasons of fiery speeches and also slogan-shouting under a green flag with a crescent moon. Because of my association with the Rizvi family I could understand their Urdu vocabulary, and what I could make out was that Islam was in grave danger and Pakistan was their ultimate goal. More than half a century has gone by since I last saw those scenes connected with Indian politics, and they are still fresh in my memory.

For the first time after coming to Delhi, we were on friendly terms with another family and it did not matter if these friends belonged to the aristocratic household of a Mughal city. In Agra as well as in Delhi both the families often went for day-long picnics to Fatehpur Sikri, Qutb Minar or the Lodi Garden. For me, photography was an important activity in all our trips. It was difficult if not impossible to imagine that, soon, Rizvi Sahib along with his entire family including an ageing father, would be flung to distant Dhaka in East Pakistan, now an independent country called Bangladesh. Decades later, when I saw the film *Garam*

Hawa by MS Sathyu, the memory of our happy days in Delhi, as well as at Rizvi Sahib's ancient haveli at Rui Mandi of Agra, came back like a wonderful but distant dream.

At last, on June 3, in 1947, all uncertainties about the political future affecting British India were over. Lord Mountbatten announced, on behalf of the British Government, that India would soon be partitioned into two independent countries.

Next morning when the morning paper arrived with that important news, my father threw the paper away and shouted that this decision to partition India into two countries would spell disaster for Hindus and Muslims. We grabbed the crumpled paper and read anxiously that, though India would at last be free from British rule, many of our good friends might have to leave New Delhi for good. In the first week of August 1947, Rizvi Sahib came alone to our house to bid us farewell. He had already sent away his family members to Agra and, after eating a farewell dinner prepared by my mother, he rushed out of our flat with tears streaming down his face. We never met him again.

Years later, in 1954, a letter arrived from Lahore in Pakistan. Rizvi Sahib wrote that he and his family members were delighted to see an illustrated feature, done by my brother and me, on the palace of Deeg. The palace happened to be located in his ancestral state, Bharatpur.

Chapter 7

Different Wavelengths

Flypast, August 15, 1947

Different Wavelengths

It is lucky that I could click a reasonably clear picture of those fighter planes with just a box camera. It is also a wonder that the particular snapshot has survived the depredation of more than half-a-century

Proper monsoon showers were more than a month overdue on August 14, 1947, and the weather around Delhi was really hot and humid. Though there were many signs of celebration all over the capital for Independence Day, the overall mood in our flat at Mori Gate had been very much in tune with the weather outside and was far from being cheerful.

After two hundred years of British rule, India was once again about to become an independent country. But my father, who had been writing his famous autobiography those days, had his own radical view about the partition of India, as well as the final end of British rule. He was not inclined to allow us to witness the historic Independence Day celebration scheduled for the next day. And even to hear Pandit Nehru's address, 'Tryst With Destiny', that midnight appeared to be difficult, if not impossible.

However, some time in the evening my cousin Krishna, who was spending her holidays with us, managed to get the sanction at last to see the celebration and to hear Pandit Nehru's address at the stroke of midnight on August 14. Krishnadi, as we called her, was very keen on politics even at that young age of sixteen. Years later, Professor Krishna Bose became a prominent member of the Indian Parliament as well as the chairperson of an important parliamentary committee.

For me, the first Independence Day celebration was a good opportunity to record this memorable event with a little box camera. The flypast by many airforce planes and the flood-lighting of public buildings of New Delhi were exciting subjects. But, at the late hour of that evening, it proved almost impossible to be able to buy even a single roll of the required photographic film.

Instead of crying over spilt milk, we youngsters were determined to make the best use of the situation. The main problem that confronted us that night was the eagerly-awaited address of Prime Minister Jawaharlal Nehru. It was difficult for us to go down to Parliament House in the middle of that night and listen to the famous speech. The other alternative was to listen to the direct relay on a radio set.

But at our flat in the P&O Building there was none available and though my father was a senior officer at the All India Radio, he had his own views about radio sets. Unfortunately, radio receivers of his high expectations were neither easily available, nor could we afford them. So I had no way other than to suggest that we should go down to Mrs Pinto's flat, and try to hear the historic broadcast on her ordinary Murphy set. Since elderly Mrs Pinto with her two sons and a daughter-in-law were going down to Parliament House, she readily allowed the use of her radio, and our problem for that night was solved.

Finally, Krishnadi and I, who were the only ones to remain awake till the midnight of August 14, listened to Jawaharlal Nehru's famous speech. Mrs Pinto's good old radio received every cadence of Pandit Nehru's voice with the utmost clarity and when I hear a replay of the same speech on television or radio today it sounds like a pale copy of the original heard in 1947.

On August 15, 1947, when the sun had risen behind Kashmere Gate, it was a ball of fire diffused with dust. The thick curtain of pale dust thrown up by thousands of men, women and children, all marching towards New Delhi, made every scene of that historic day appear like a painting by Van Gogh. Our team of three boys and a girl, all in their teens, also set off early towards New Delhi. We were determined to face all odds to see the important events of that epoch-making day. The third boy in our party was my cousin Sanat Dutta Majumdar, who was a few months younger to me and had come to Delhi from a small town in East Bengal to improve his health.

After trying to get into many forms of transport, mechanical or animal, our group walked through the streets of Old Delhi and finally reached Princes Square, called Vijay Chowk after India achieved its independence. By then that vast square was swarming with thousands of people and on the twin flagpoles of each tower on the Secretariat the British flags of the Union Jack were still flying, but seemed to be rather tired and dejected with very little life.

Soon the horse-drawn coach of the last Viceroy, with mounted guards galloping away on both sides, rolled down the slope of New Delhi's Raisina Hill and Lord and Lady Mountbatten waved with enthusiasm at the wildly-cheering crowd. The swarming mass of men and women, often with little children in their arms, seemed to be touching the state coach and also patting some of those horses of the guards. Yet, there was not a single sign of ill feeling or trouble at those last few minutes of the British rule. Today, such free and unrestricted scenes at Vijay Chowk are difficult to imagine even after fifty years of democracy.

Some minutes later, when the British Governor-General entered the central hall of Parliament House to transfer power, a Howitzer cannon boomed across Princes Square. And India was once again free. As Union Jacks got replaced with the Indian tricolours, and everyone was cheering with joy, suddenly Krishnadi saw a police horse with its teeth exposed and a slobbering mouth right above her head. My cousin, even though clad in a traditional khadi sari, sprinted across the road in a flash, and just vanished into the vast crowd assembled there. We, the three gallant boys, had a real tough time fishing her out of that sea of humanity. At last, under the hot sun of that August noon, we

King Edward's statue, 1950

began to walk all the way to Mori Gate, dog tired, but in real high spirits.

Though we had to return to our house in Old Delhi, some of the evening events after the unfurling of the National Flag were bound to be exciting. A display of fireworks scheduled that night at Ramlila Ground outside the old city was making me restless for a roll of photographic film. However, around four that afternoon, there was a literal bolt from the blue; it proved the well-known saying, "If there is a will, there is [definitely] a way."

Just as we were getting ready to march out once again, a young man who looked like a student appeared at the front door of our flat and told us that he had been asked by Professor DK Sanyal, a very good friend of my father and also our house guest, to escort us to India Gate grounds. Dilip Kaka, as we called him, seemed to have arranged for a place near the main ceremony site. And not only that, he had a message especially for me, that I could take the fresh roll of film lying unused in his suitcase.

Compared to our morning experiences, the tonga ride to Central Vista was quite comfortable, and with our aunt, Krishnadi's mother, coming along with us, the financial aspect was taken care of. But, to our disappointment, the proper viewing of the flag-hoisting ceremony was not possible. It is difficult to remember who did the actual unfurling, Lord Louis Mounbatten or Prime Minister Nehru. We heard the 25-pounder guns once again and at that very moment a squadron of Spitfire fighters, followed by Liberator bombers, did the very first flypast over Central Vista. It is lucky that I could click a reasonably clear picture of those fighter planes with just a box camera. It is also a wonder that the particular snapshot has survived the depredation of more than half-a-century.

After the main event at Princes Park, we walked towards Parliament Street down Ashoka Road, and on reaching the old Town Hall building, opposite Jantar Mantar, all of us flopped down on the cool and green lawn of that public building. Late in the evening, when flood-lights were finally switched on, my time exposure shot of that unique clock tower of New Delhi could only be taken by supporting the camera on a couple of bricks.

This unique clock tower along with the Town Hall has disappeared from Parliament Street. and the photograph taken on that historic day is perhaps the only record in existence.

However, all the euphoria seen on that first Independence Day was rather short lived, and got shattered in less than two weeks.

On a hot afternoon towards the end of August 1947, my brother and I were giving cycling lessons to both Krishnadi and Zubeida Baji, who had been staying with our family for a few days because of some rumours heard by her husband Muthahir Khan. But Mori Gate that afternoon and also Nicholson Road were serene and quiet. Many of the shopkeepers, including our cycle wallah, was dozing in his red fez cap. All of a sudden we heard my mother from our front verandah shouting at us to rush home, and that was when we came to notice that the bazaar inside Mori Gate was strangely quiet. Once at home we were told that curfew had been declared and there were reports of sporadic trouble inside the old city. That evening our faithful attendant, Dhanuk Dhari, who also worked as a peon at the All India Radio Office, did not return home.

Next morning, when curfew had been lifted, and all appeared quiet around Mori Gate, my father asked us to go down to Broadcasting House to enquire about Dhanu. He was engrossed in a crucial chapter of his book and was not inclined to move. We two brothers, accompanied by Krishnadi, set out immediately for New Delhi on three cycles hired from a nearby shop. Our route was through the grain mart of Naya Bazaar near Lahore Gate and then on to Ajmere Gate by the somewhat ill-reputed GB Road. While cycling along that particular road we found it to be strangely deserted and yet all the balconies were packed with many women and a few men. Everyone there was gaping at us, the three odd-looking youngsters, including a girl in her teens dressed in a cotton sari. Noticing the attention from the floors above, my brother abruptly ordered our cousin to adjust her sari, which he deduced was the main reason for the undue attention to our group. Our cousin complied with that curt request promptly, but narrowly escaped an awkward accident with her bike.

All of a sudden, a group of army men rushed out of a wayside lane with pointed guns and after blowing their whistles ordered us to stop. One of those men, who appeared to be an officer, was rather surprised to see our young age as well as disturbed faces. He ordered us to get out of that area, firmly, but with concern. It seemed that there had been serious trouble in many parts of the old city and the army had to resort to firing to disperse an unruly mob, with fatal results. Some of those soldiers in khaki

■ NDMC Building, August 15, 1947

kept a careful watch on us till we got out of the city near Ajmere Gate.

Once on Thompson Road we cycled like mad, but after coming up the steep slope of Minto Bridge our didi could go no further, and just collapsed on the pavement, exhausted. I really do not remember how I managed to hire a tonga near Odeon Cinema. After loading all the cycles, as well as ourselves, on the horse-drawn cart, we began an anxious and long ride to Mori Gate through some of the curfew-free roads and rather safe localities.

From the evening of that day hell broke loose all over Delhi and when, armed with an official pass, my father tried to reach his office he saw the looting of many shops at Connaught Place. He returned home totally devastated after seeing many scenes of destruction all over the city. On the same day Pandit Nehru tried to stop many looters at Connaught Place by beating people with a police lathi. Then one day we heard the staccato firing of machine-guns coming from an old suburb called Sabzi Mandi. When I told my father that a gun-battle was probably going on there, he flared up at once and gave me a solid verbal bashing. But my information, which was picked up from a ration shop near a mosque, proved to be correct.

For many nights, whenever we went up to the terrace to sleep, we could notice fires blazing all around Delhi. Towards the old city near Phatak Habash Khan we could also see many cloth balls set on fire being tossed from house-to-house in a frenzy of violence. There were continuous rattles of gun firing from the direction of Dufferin Bridge and Queen's Road. Often stray bullets whistled overhead, and when moving to our flat down below, we had to take the precaution of crawling on all fours. Since it was not safe for Zubeida Baji to be taken to her home in New Delhi, my mother dressed her up as a Bengali bride in a sari, and even put a vermilion mark on her forehead, to indicate that she was a married girl from a Hindu family.

In the third week of September 1947 our house had become suddenly quiet. My aunt and cousin Krishna, accompanied by Professor Sanyal, left for Kolkata. Zubeida Baji was escorted to a refugee camp in Purana Qila by her husband. With the curfew order strictly enforced, the entire area around our house was totally silent throughout the day. One of those uncanny evenings we were startled to hear the loud-throated roar of a lion coming from the direction of the Ridge, and we wondered seriously if Charles Trevelyan's report on seeing lions near Delhi was true.

Next morning, as soon as the curfew hours were over, we rushed out of Mori Gate and finally spotted a young lioness inside a cage at the SPCA premise on Boulevard Road. The animal appeared to be famished and so we went back home to ask my mother for some omelettes made with war-surplus powdered eggs. Mother just laughed us off, and told us to get lost in no uncertain terms. But on our return to that animal hospital we found the hungry lioness was being fed with a freshly-killed maimed horse. Since the regular supply of meat was proving to be difficult and expensive, the lioness was shot after a few days and the roar silenced around Mori Gate for all times to come.

Towards the end of October 1947, all areas of Delhi began to change rapidly because of the havoc caused by the partition of India and the resulting influx of Punjabi refugees. But one traditional area inside the old city remained largely unchanged and that was the junk market at the Jama Masjid. And, as chance would have it, I had an opportunity to visit that market for making a crystal radio set.

When many Pathan tribal men began to plunder Kashmir, and nearly reached Srinagar, we began to hear the constant roar of aeroplanes flying overhead with military supplies. What happened is now history, but for me to wait for the newspaper next morning to get all the news was becoming difficult, if not impossible. Also to hang around the neighbours' radio sets was proving to be rather embarrassing as well as a sheer waste of time. So I started a project to build a simple crystal radio on my own.

The amount of ten rupees needed for all the components, including a pair of headphones, was raised from the cash-present given by Rizvi Sahib. But to go near the war-surplus market required an escort. At last, one Saturday afternoon, after persuading Dhanuk Dhari Mandal to put on his government livery, complete with an impressive turban, I managed to get an official escort. As for myself, I carried a sherwani, which had been given to us as a parting present from Mutahir Bhai, and after crossing the jeweller's mart of Dariba Kalan in Chandni Chowk, I put on that garment like an overcoat. The final result of that correctly-uniformed expedition was that I got all the components right. After a week of effort, the signature tune of the All India Radio composed for a violin came through loud and clear.

Some months later, on a dark evening of January 30, 1948, I clamped on the headphones and switched on my little wireless set. But to my great surprise no voice or music could be heard through the headset. I was expecting some English or Hindi news, if not a relay from Mahatma Gandhi's daily prayer meetings.

As I fiddled with the tuning knob, suddenly a voice broke the silence, and I heard clearly, "We announce with great regret that Mr Mohandas Karamchand Gandhi has just been shot by an assassin and is presumably dead!" I could just not believe what I heard and pressed both the earphones close to my ears.

After hearing the same announcement no less than three times, I finally tore off the instrument from my head and ran across to the next room, where my parents were present. "Gandhiji has been shot dead," I screamed. While my mother jumped up from her chair and called out to Mrs Pinto to switch on her radio, my father rushed into my little radio nook and asked for the headset. In a few minutes all radio sets in our locality were announcing the sad news.

Late in the evening of that sorrowful day, I heard Pandit Jawaharlal Nehru as well as his deputy, Sardar Patel, on my crystal set. Pandit Nehru's voice, as I remember, was choked with emotion, and as he spoke the famous lines,

"The light has gone out of our lives," he almost broke down in tears. In contrast, Sardar Patel's speech was stoic, yet powerful.

While listening to the two stalwarts of the government as well as of the Congress Party, the old memory of my first vision of Mahatma Gandhi way back on an early winter evening of 1937 came flashing across my mind.

I had my first glimpse of Gandhiji while standing at a door of 1, Woodburn Park in Kolkata, and saw not only him, but also Netaji Subhas Bose, and Pandit Nehru, too. The memory of that historical group is still vivid. I remember the dark complexion of Gandhiji's bare torso as well as his two prominent ears.

Returning to that grief-stricken day of 1948, I learnt from my home-made radio that the funeral procession would start from Birla House, where Gandhiji had breathed his last. After reaching Raj Ghat on the banks of the Yamuna, the cremation ceremony was scheduled in the evening as the sun went down. I also came to know from an announcement that there would be a continuous commentary all through the day. Not only that, the broadcast would cover the entire route. So instead of rushing out like many of our neighbours and friends, I made up my mind to sit at home and hear what my father's colleague, Melville de Mello, had to say through my little radio.

At about eleven in the morning I heard that the cortege was about to start from Birla House, and everyone from Lord Louis Mountbatten, Pandit Nehru, to thousands of men, women and even children of Delhi thronged to Albuquerque Road, now called Tees January Marg, all along the route right up to the now famous Raj Ghat.

It was perhaps somewhat ironical that an army weapon carrier was used to carry the mortal remains of Mahatma Gandhi, an apostle of peace.

On the very last day of January 1948, the entire procession route, the Central Vista, along with all other important roads, and the rail overbridge on Mathura Road, had gigantic crowds, which Delhi had never seen before.

It was good that I did not try to go out with my camera, though I was very much inclined to. Many of the veteran photographers such as Margaret Bourke-White and Henry Cartier Bresson had a real tough time working in that crowd. However, the radio commentary was really vivid and Melville de Mello could convey very well the grief and the solemn mood that was prevailing all over Delhi.

Before sunset, the cortege finally reached Rajghat just outside the old city wall near Delhi Gate. In those days, the riverbank and Raj Ghat were wild and deserted places. The only sign of human life was the lone chimney of Delhi's single powerhouse some distance away. Just as the evening mist began to gather over the Yamuna and the sun was about to set, the army buglers sounded the last post and the funeral pyre was lit. As the strain of Gandhiji's favourite hymn 'Ram Dhun' began to rise with a crescendo, it became impossible for people to hold back their tears. That was the sad, solemn destiny of a legendary human being called Mahatma Gandhi.

Chapter 8

Rewinding History

Lodi Tomb, 1948

Rewinding History

When we climbed up the steep staircase to the base of the main tomb, we saw the total transformation of that picturesque monument into a squalid and congested slum created by the tragic partition of the Indian continent

For many of us living in Delhi, 1948 had begun on a sombre mood. There were shades of grey all around us. The aftermath of the Partition left us saddened. We found it difficult to come to terms with the changes that had occurred in our lives.

While going on an overnight visit to Agra to show the Taj Mahal to our cousin Sanat, I caught a glimpse of the train carrying the ashes of Mahatma Gandhi. That train was standing at the special platform of New Delhi station where only Viceroys and other top dignitaries of the British days used to board. Agra at that time was strangely quiet and passing through its familiar streets I sadly missed the presence of the Rizvi family. There were unfamiliar men and also women seen in the streets. All the camaraderie in chaste Urdu, heard only a year earlier in the lanes and streets of Agra, had vanished. In Delhi this transformation was even more pronounced and disturbing. A few days before Sanat went back to his hometown in East Bengal, we were sent to the old Ghantewale's shop in Chandni Chowk to buy some of the typical sweets of Delhi. After reaching the Fountain, we found the Sunehri Masjid to be strangely deserted. It was here that Nadir Shah had sat under the golden domes of that mosque to order one of the worst massacres that Delhi had seen. Under the same mosque some of the shops, which sold sola topees, or pith hats, as well as bedrolls and suitcases were ransacked and partially burnt. As we were regular customers, to see the shops in that condition was definitely distressing.

While passing the domed building of Hardinge Library in Queen's Garden or Company Bagh, I saw that a well-known cinema house just outside that garden gate was completely gutted. Only at odd places some posters of movie stars were smiling down grotesquely from the grim walls of that burnt building.

We had to walk across a railway footbridge called Kauria Pul, which was famous for its beggars. But on that day nearly all beggars, including burqa-clad women holding Urdu messages scribbled on cardboard pieces, had disappeared and their places were taken by young Sikh men selling fruits and cheap trinkets. Earlier, from the same bridge, I often watched all types of steam engines at the busy loco-shed of the Delhi junction. Even there, many of those coal-fed engines had no smoke or steam visible around them and some of the drivers and firemen, with characteristic beards and turbans, appeared to be missing.

After coming down from Kauria Pul, we cousins walked down Hamilton Road towards Dufferin Bridge. Hamilton Road, which was laid-out after the railways reached Delhi, was a curious mixture of the old and the new. Right from its starting point near Delhi's General Post Office till Pul Mithai and St. Stephen's Hospital, Hamilton Road had railway yards running along its entire length. This road was also a section of the original Grand Trunk Road. One curious milepost near Dufferin Bridge showed that Kolkata was 902 miles from that spot. Opposite the rail yard this British road had a mixture of buildings, which were quite dilapidated.

On a sudden impulse, Sanat and I decided to walk through Ganda Nalah not only to take a shortcut but also to see the many changes brought about by the partition of our country. What we saw was far from cheerful and made us feel somewhat odd that we were carrying baskets of sweets. Everywhere around that old lane there were refugee families who had arrived from West Punjab. They spoke in a strange dialect.

Only at the end of Ganda Nalah, near Mori Gate, did we see a few elderly men with white beards and white caps. They were whispering and what I gathered from their muted conversation, fifty-five years ago, is still fresh in my memory. They were saying that the cruel turn of fate was making them leave their Ganda Nalah, which had been their abode from the time of their late fathers and grandfathers.

One morning, when we went to see off Sanat and my uncle, we found that every train that was arriving from Punjab had thousands of people, even on top of the carriages. The stink all around the old Delhi station was something that could not be imagined and not a single square foot of empty space was available on any platform of that big railway junction. To push in our uncle and cousin into their reserved compartment was a feat not to be forgotten.

A few days later, we had to face our first bereavement after coming to Delhi. One night our faithful dog Rex died after vomiting blood. Towards the last few months of his life, Rex had not been well and went for his walks with a good deal of reluctance. Ever since the post-Independence problems started in Delhi, we could not give him the regular quota of milk and meat. The scrambled powdered egg he was compelled to take with rice could hardly sustain him. In addition, the regular veterinary doctor of SPCA had been a Pathan gentleman with a long beard, who could no longer be traced. It was not possible to give proper treatment to our good old Rex.

All of a sudden, a few days before my birthday in February 1948, a complete stranger came to visit my father for an article on British foreign policy and to listen to European classical music on our gramophone. He had heard about my father's interests from Professor DK Sanyal, at their shared residence in Daryagunj. There was such a shortage of proper accommodation in Delhi at that time that two or more families

■ Atgah Khan Tomb, Nizamuddin, 1949

often had to share a single flat. Pranab Kumar Guha was in his middle twenties, and had just returned from Oxford to join the Publications Division of the Government of India at the Old Secretariat building in Civil Lines.

On that particular day he had a Voightlander camera slung from his shoulder and from his talk I guessed that he was really serious about photography. Though he had come to meet my father for a definite purpose, we became very close friends in spite of an age difference of more than a decade.

If there had been anyone who had helped me all along the thirty-seven years that I knew him, it was this bespectacled young man with a studious expression. Our mutual interest in serious photography as well as the desire to know all the historic sites of Delhi brought us very close. Within a few weeks of our first meeting we began to go out on Sundays to many of the picturesque sites of Delhi such as Hauz Khas, Qutb Minar and Humayun's Tomb as well as Delhi's picnic spot on the Yamuna, called Okhla.

The choice of locations for our photographic excursions was dictated more by the availability of Delhi's bus routes. Some of the buses with numbers such as 17, 18 and 19, started from a stand inside Queen's Garden near the Fountain of Chandni Chowk. We kept our excursions' plans flexible, according to the particular bus which would be standing at that stand and if any sitting place happened to be available. Route number 17 used to go up to Mehrauli after a brief stop at the enclosure of Qutb. The other two routes in their numerical order went up to Okhla and Lodi Road quarters, respectively. Since all these bus routes were considered long distance services, the buses were built with a low roof and no one was allowed to stand. I had just touched five feet

Okhla barrage, 1948

that time and Pranab Babu was only a couple of inches more. So for us to get into those low vehicles swiftly and make a disorderly exit did not pose any problem.

One Sunday morning in the early spring of 1948, we set off for a day's excursion towards the Qutb Minar with our two cameras. We had to wait at an informal queue for less than thirty minutes and considered ourselves lucky. The 'Bedford' bus trundled out of Delhi Gate quite smoothly, and after passing Feroz Shah Kotla on the left, and Delhi's central jail to the right, passed through a kikar tree forest and a lonely, ruined mosque standing on a mound next to what is now known as IP Estate or ITO. Little could I imagine then that in less than a decade I should be working there at what is now called the School of Planning and Architecture (SPA). Later, all bungalows on Hardinge Avenue were hidden by thick clumps of trees and only the two-storeyed residence of Muslim League leader Liaquat Ali Khan, who became the first Prime Minister of Pakistan, was visible. The building was to become the Pakistan High Commissioner's residence.

Our bus smoothly drove past Safdarjung's Tomb and the sleepy village called Yusuf Sarai. Just as Moth-ki-Masjid came into view, the vehicle came to a halt with a grinding sound. There were three or four village urchins sitting on a nearby culvert and they signalled, rather gleefully, that something under the bus was broken and had fallen down. Our conductor, after a cursory glance under the bus, announced with perfect calm that the bus would go no further and just sat down under the shade of a wayside neem tree to smoke some locally-made bidis. For us, the two camera enthusiasts, it was a bit of an anti-climax, so we decided to walk up to Hauz Khas first rather than the Qutb Minar.

To recognise the narrow branch road to Hauz Khas was hardly a problem. For, just off the main road to Mehrauli, there were two tombs called Dadi Poti (grandmother, grandchild) by local villagers. One of them had an unusual lantern on the top of its dome and served as a landmark to the ancient madrassa at Hauz Khas, or the Royal Reservoir. Originally, the complex was created by Alauddin Khilji as a royal resort. Later Feroz Shah Tughlaq developed it as a royal seat of learning around that beautiful tank. He liked the place so much that he even decided to construct his own last resting place at a prominent corner at Hauz Khas.

When Pranab and I stood at the small terrace just outside that tomb, looking towards the lake, the view right up to the horizon and dargah at Mohammadpur was really breathtaking. We took good care, while taking pictures almost in a trance. I had read in Percival Spear's book, which I had got as a birthday present, to be careful and not fall overboard at that spot. Many years later, a prominent architect, Habib-ur-Rehman, was seriously injured after an accidental fall when showing a foreign friend around this area.

After taking some interesting shots of the Hauz Khas ruins, we came to a really tranquil rural scene just outside the entrance gate. Over there, the village elders were sitting, next to the road, on string cots called charpai and smoking village hookahs in lazy puffs. Many little children scampered around them in mud and dust, with no one to take them seriously. Women in heavy lehngas, their faces covered in chaddars like masks, were either washing cattle or busy patting cow-dung cakes on mud walls. It was impossible to imagine that we were only a few miles south of a capital city.

Of course, today, with the entire village transformed by boutiques, craft shops and expensive eating places, very few can recall the Hauz Khas village of the olden days. At last, we managed to reach the Qutb enclosure in a shared tonga. Since we had eaten all our home-made sandwiches as a mid-morning snack, Pranab Babu generously offered to take me to the red sandstone Qutb bungalow for lunch. However, we had a disappointment in store. The good old khansama, the head cook who was famous for his chicken cutlets, usually called fowl cutlets by fellow Bengalis from Kolkata, had disappeared after Partition.

Gujjar girl, Hauz Khas village, 1951

All we got there were some oily omelettes, on soggy toasts, with watery tea. Moreover, the cost of that disappointing lunch, at five rupees for two, was indeed quite a sum those days.

To improve our mood, we set off towards the Jamali Kamali Masjid to find a totally new angle to Delhi's famous landmark, the Qutb Minar. After keeping the British-made eyesore of a chhatri on our right, we walked on to a grove of large neem trees. There we found a natural arch formed by two old trees and the view of the old minar was truly unique. Later, even near Alai Darwaza, I could find a view which was so unusual that though taken with only a box camera, it was published in my first photo- feature in 1952. Climbing on to the top of the Qutb Minar, even on a Sunday afternoon, was hardly a problem those days and the view from the top on that clear winter day was truly unique. Though the countryside all around the Qutb was rocky and dotted with tombs and old ruins, at a great distance, the white domes of the Jama Masjid, along with the government buildings on Raisina Hill, were etched against the blue sky like an old Canaletto painting.

Once again I managed to take a complete picture of the ruined mosque. In that old photograph we cannot see more than three or four human beings around the iron pillar. At the twilight of that winter evening, when we began to walk through the Mehrauli village to the bus stand near Adham Khan's tomb, there was hardly any light visible and the place seemed to have gone to sleep quite early.

After reaching Mori Gate when the night was quite young I heard the noise of a big commotion behind our building. At the end of our lane, where it almost touched Ganda Nalah, there was a large unfinished house. Its owner was a rich Muslim merchant, who was missing. The improvised entry gate of that half-completed structure was torn down and not less than ten or fifteen families occupied these rooms. Nearly all of those refugee families were from a prosperous town in West Punjab called Sargodha. We came to know the details from a bright young man who had taken shelter there along with his brother's family and, within a few months, came to see my father for a job in the All India Radio. The late Satya Paul Sakhuja was already a holder of two Master's degrees and was teaching at a college in one of the West Punjab towns.

He had spotted us practising the viola and the violin on our front verandah, while out for his morning ablutions in the moat outside

Many shades, 1948

Mori Gate. The building he had moved into with more than fifty people did not have a single working toilet. Desperate for a job and money, he had enquired at Mrs Pinto's press and was told about my father's position as a senior government officer in the All India Radio. He mustered up courage and walked into our flat as a complete stranger and soon became a close friend of everyone, including my father who accepted him as a welcome protégé.

Satya Paul did manage to find a reasonable job not at the radio station but at the National Archives. He became a staunch admirer of my father's writings even before his well-known autobiography was published.

Returning to my next camera excursion around Delhi with Pranab Guha, our trip to Humayun's Tomb was a sad experience indeed.

On that day the bus ride on route number 18 was remarkably easy and incident-free. As we walked through the picturesque gate, shaped like an open embrace, an offensive smell greeted us. There were many children in dirty clothes, and they were squatting freely over dry water channels all around that beautiful tomb. Modesty, of course, dictated that adults use the thick flowering bushes of oleanders and other shrubs growing next to the walls surrounding the picturesque tomb. When we climbed up the steep staircase to the base of the main tomb, we saw the total transformation of that picturesque monument into a squalid and congested slum created by the tragic partition of the Indian sub-continent. Every possible space in that noble building was swarming with people, men, women and young kids of all ages and sizes.

There was also every form of daily activity such as cooking, eating, sleeping, going on. No one took the slightest notice of us, two total strangers, and we were so overwhelmed by the scenes of human misery around us that we walked out without clicking a single picture.

I could well imagine what that picturesque building must have looked like during the very last days of the Mughal rule, when the old emperor Bahadur Shah Zafar took refuge there with his queen Zinat Mahal and a large entourage, including many sons.

For months together after that depressing experience we left all historic buildings alone. All of us living around Mori Gate and on Nicholson Road began to see similar scenes such as at Humayun's Tomb right before our house. Almost overnight hundreds of refugee families built their shacks of rusted tin and worm-eaten planks under every alcove of the old city wall, as well as on the narrow rampart above the arches. The entire length of Nicholson Road, once really clean and smart, had been turned into a bustling slum by people who had no control over the miseries created by the politicians of India, Pakistan and England.

Since our visit to Humayun's Tomb and some other old monuments occupied by refugees was far from happy, a week or two later we went to see Laurence Olivier's *Hamlet*. This proved to be a stunning experience for me. At the foyer of Regal Cinema, among many intellectuals and English teachers of Delhi who had gathered there, Pranab Babu introduced me to a young Bengali couple, Mr and Mrs OK Ghosh. After seeing the brilliant performance and the black-and-white photography, we went to a restaurant, which had started more or less as an ice-cream parlour and a popular meeting-place for tea. For me, meeting Mr Ghosh and his wife Rekhadi, was as memorable as seeing *Hamlet* and eating my first triple sundae.

By the time India's second Independence Day had been celebrated and Pandit Jawaharlal Nehru had made his annual speech from the ramparts of Red Fort, Delhi had turned into a peaceful capital with tremendous zeal. Many of the new refugee colonies, sponsored and built by the Rehabilitation Ministry, came up in the outskirts of the capital. While the general mass of people began to move to the asbestos-roofed nagars such as Lajpat, Rajinder and Patel, the rich merchants, including those from Delhi, began to buy scrublands dotted with old ruins in places such as Jor Bagh, Sunder Nagar and Golf Links.

The situation at that time had a strong resemblance to the immense building activities the old city and Civil Lines had seen at the turn of the nineteenth century. The Government officers who could not be accommodated in quarters planned by Lutyens took up their residences mostly in the Western Extension Area of Karol Bagh, on the other side of New Delhi's Ridge. At that time Pranab Guha married a charming young lady, whom we called Sujata Didi. She was also from Bangladesh. Her original ancestral place was probably Noakhali, where Mahatma Gandhi had undertaken a pad yatra, or a walking tour, to quench the flames of the communal riots in 1946. Pranab at that time was editing a magazine called *The Foreign Review* of the Publications Division at the Old Secretariat and had to share a flat with Mr and Mrs Ghosh at Karol Bagh. I, along with my brothers, was a regular invader in that flat and because of our interest in classical music and photography, we received a lot of encouragement from both the families.

It was in the house of OK Ghosh in Karol Bagh that I first met my guru, T Kasinath, an eminent photographer of great excellence and the chief photo editor in the Publications Division. For fifty long years he was always there to guide me in my career. He put me on the right track as a photographer and also as a teacher of visual communication.

Part 3

Shadows

Chapter 9

Yesterday's Delhi

Tughlaqabad, 1950

Yesterday's Delhi

Though the New Year of 1951 was still more than six hours away, I could not help but take two important resolutions about my future: to appear at the coming High School Examination as a private candidate and to start photographing the historic monuments of Delhi

I stood on the roof of Vijay Mandal, a unique stone building from the Tughlaq era, on the last evening of December 1950. I saw the sun going down behind the old ruins of Mohammadpur. Standing on that high point I could see a range of historical buildings from the Qutb and Tughlaqabad to the white glistening dome of Safdarjung's Tomb. At a short distance, the Moth-ki-Masjid stood alone among the yellow and green mustard fields touching the village called Yusuf Sarai. The sombre form of the Begumpur Masjid was also visible at that twilight hour, with its high entrance arch and numerous conical domes. A thin veil of acrid-smelling cowdung smoke, rising from many of the hearths at Begumpur village, began to cover the rugged landscape around me.

Though the New Year of 1951 was still more than six hours away, I could not help but take two important resolutions about my future. One was to appear at the coming High School Examination as a private candidate and do well. In the second, I resolved to start photographing all the historic monuments of Delhi as best as possible and to explore the possibilities of publishing them in newspapers and magazines.

At that time I was nearly eighteen and not having gone to school for even a single day did create an imbalance in my formal education. Also, with my father's serious illness, my future prospects were not exactly bright or cheerful. So, in order to earn a living while studying I had resolved to turn my interest in photography and also better-than-average knowledge of the historic city of Delhi into some use. The shadows of the setting sun were witness to these resolutions. The moment was a decisive one for me. For, I had just chosen my path.

Suraj Kund, 1960

Today, a question about Vijay Mandal would perhaps be relevant in a television quiz conducted by a mega star. But way back, till the mid-fifties, it would have been impossible to miss that unusual Tughlaq building, while trotting along in a tonga to Qutb Minar. In those days every historic site in Delhi, well-known or obscure, had a red sandstone signpost which pointed towards it from the main road. Vijay Mandal along with the Begampur Masjid could hardly escape one's attention. It was another matter that a dust track winding among dry fields would lead to those sites often surrounded by villages that had not changed for centuries.

On that December evening of 1950 all of us, including my father and a group of family friends, had gone for a day-long picnic, starting at Suraj Kund. After our first visit to that remote and ancient monument from the Hindu era we stopped at Tughlaqabad Fort for lunch. The unique Vijay Mandal along with the Begumpur Masjid was our last halt and a stopover for some tea or coffee. Since my father had never touched tea it was imperative that only coffee should be served that evening, along with cucumber and cheese sandwiches.

Our picnic-cum-sightseeing group was extremely varied in age as well as family background and profession. Apart from my parents and we three brothers, there were two gentlemen from the ancient Hindu town of Varanasi. Jyotish Chandra Bhattacharya and his uncle, Pandit Gopal Chandra Bhattacharya, were running a family business of ayurvedic medicines from a haveli in Bazaar Sita Ram in Delhi. These two young men in their thirties, though rather traditional in their family background and in appearance, were modern in their outlook.

It was Khokada and Gopal Mama, as we called them, who provided two vintage cars for that excursion – a station wagon built sometime in the twenties on a Chevrolet chassis and an Austin Ten made in 1934, that is, a year younger to me. It was rather bold of us to have arranged that excursion to Suraj Kund, which could only be reached at that time after driving over rugged terrain with dust tracks used by bullock carts going to the old village of Anangpur. The other two young couples in our group were Mr and Mrs PK Guha and Mr and Mrs OK Ghosh. The Ghoshs had, towards the end of 1950, just moved into a new flat in a government colony, initially called Man Nagar.

On that rather cold, but sunny day, before reaching Vijay Mandal, we made our first visit to Suraj Kund. Looking at the Suraj Kund area now no one can imagine what a wild and desolate look the entire place had at that time. Having read Professor Percival Spear's book on the monuments of Delhi, we took all the warnings about visiting Suraj Kund with seriousness. As for me, who had taken history as an optional subject in my school final examinations, a visit to that ancient kund had became a necessity. In the history examination, a question on Delhi monuments used to be compulsory and the question often asked used to be on the rarely-visited Suraj Kund from the Hindu period.

All of us had gathered first in front of Humayun's Tomb, at the junction of Lodi and Mathura Road. The roundabout had a unique blue-tiled tomb from the Mughal period located here and served as a meeting point for many of my trips. Soon after loading the motor vehicles with more than one tiffin carrier, a few thermos flasks and a cane lunch basket of ample size, we began our drive towards Badarpur.

In those days there was not a single flyover or an underpass all along that route on Mathura Road. As chance would have it, every time we came across a level crossing, and they were no less than three, most of them were closed. Since our old cars had no working self-starters, every time when we stopped at a railway crossing some us had to jump out and crank the starter handle of the vintage Chevrolet or pushstart the good old Austin Ten.

Mathura Road till the early fifties of the last century was quite narrow and not very much different from what Bishop Heber had described in his travels to Delhi in 1824. The general landscape was rocky, desolate and dotted with old ruins, which were mostly tombs. The occasional villages such as Jangpura, Bhogal, or even Nizamuddin, stood usually isolated among dusty fields. The village of Badarpur, too, though located on Mathura Road itself, was no exception. The village was also well-fortified with rugged stone walls complete with a massive wooden gate to keep out the marauders. On the main road, a few small teashops, along with a lone tonga or two, completed the entire village scene.

Here our cars had to take a turn towards the lonely Badarpur-Mehrauli Road. As the railway level crossing was once again closed, some of us were rather glad to jump out of our vehicles, which were packed like sardine cans. Only a short distance from the crossing was the sleepy Tughlaqabad station, with not a single soul to be seen on the platform. On my first visit to Tughlaqabad in 1943 with my father and an uncle, we had to alight on that same platform after a journey of three long hours from Old Delhi junction. Later we had to walk two miles to the ruined citadel on foot.

This time our old carriers behaved reasonably well and within an hour of starting from Nizamuddin Aulia's dargah on Mathura Road we finally arrived at a solitary village temple with a well, called Lal Kuan. Here, a stop had become an urgent necessity because our vintage cars not only consumed petrol by gallons, but were also a thirsty lot for water in their radiators, particularly when driven on the cross-country roads of that period. From Lal Kuan, or the Red Well, a solitary red stone signboard pointed towards Suraj Kund, which was still about two miles away, across a rocky and desolate landscape. The road, which our old vehicles had to struggle on, was really a deeply-rutted dust track flanked by boulders and scraggy hills. After half-an-hour of alternate gear-changing and racing of our car engines all we could do was to call out, "Abandon cars", and trudge all the way to the old kund, or tank, on foot.

No one from our group had seen Suraj Kund before. Suddenly, the vast amphitheatre of stone steps along with the green water of that huge tank, glittering under the morning sun, flashed into our view.

After climbing up the slope of a low ridge all of us were thrilled by the first sight of that ancient monument, which in the eleventh century was probably the sun temple of the Rajput king, Anang Pal Tomar. The entire rocky landscape was dotted with dhak or flame of the forest trees and no trace of human habitation could be found. Only when we began our walk towards the old bundh and the chhatri near the village of Anangpur, did we meet a couple of tribal Gujjar boys with stout sticks, tending their herd of goats. After polite greetings were exchanged they told us about a leopard they had seen lurking in that scrubland. After that warning, we were rather sad to leave that beautiful lakeside dotted with date-palm trees, but resolved to come back to see all the old ruins left by Anang Pal Tomar.

It was well past lunchtime when we returned to our cars. As it had been difficult to carry the bulky load of food and drinks to Suraj Kund, our elders shifted the venue of our picnic to Tughlaqabad. After our tough experience of reaching Suraj Kund, the drive to the citadel of Ghiyas-ud-din Tughlaq was almost child's play and could be covered in less than twenty minutes. After spreading cotton durries on a stone platform inside Tughlaqbad Fort, all of us fell hungrily upon piles of food prepared by my mother and the two young ladies from our rather diverse picnic group.

The menu was unconventional and rather eclectic. To begin with we had Bengali khhichuri, a rich mixture of rice boiled with moong lentils and fried aubergine with aloo-dum cooked in no health-conscious vegetable oil, but real ghee. What followed was braised mutton with a sharp mint sauce. All that fare was eaten eagerly, accompanied by Russian salad complete with ham and egg. Finally, for drinks we had many glasses of English cider and a chilled fruit punch. There were no monkeys around Tughlaqabad fort on that particular day, and so everyone could enjoy the dessert of bananas and oranges.

After that sumptuous lunch not many in our party were inclined to go up the citadel to a high spot inside the inner sanctum of that old palace. Today, only a high mound can be seen at that location. The rest of the palace structures are gone. Yet, once this particular place was supposed to be the highest spot in historic Delhi and gave the impression of a king's power in no uncertain terms.

As for the view from that spot, it was truly unique. Whenever I got a chance to visit Tughlaqabad on a clear day, I was always ready to see that splendid spectacle of many historic buildings of Delhi, along with some of the landmarks of New Delhi.

Nearby, right next to the old Tughlaqabad fort, was the fortified tomb of Ghiyas-ud-din and his son Mohammad Tughlaq. At some distance towards the southeast, the ruins of Adilabad Fort looked as rugged as the stone-strewn desolate countryside. The only form of green visible from that high spot was a narrow ribbon of dark green trees, mainly neem, lining the road to Mehrauli. There, the tall Qutb Minar along with the octagonal tomb of Adham Khan were the main landmarks on the western horizon.

On that clear December afternoon, which now has become something of a rarity in Delhi, the view towards the north was equally interesting. The gleaming white domes of the Jami Masjid, Humayun's Tomb and Safdarjung's Tomb could all be spotted from inside Tughlaqabad fort. We could also make out the Masjid Moth and Vijay Mandal that day and decided to stop there for our evening snacks and coffee.

When we climbed down from the highest spot of that citadel and started to move towards the main water reservoir more than fifty feet deep, two monitor lizards scurried across our path. Among some of the ruined buildings we could pick up several porcupine quills. The two young ladies in our party fancied these quills so much that they immediately used them as decorative hairpins. We also passed a secret underground passage, which opened out at the far end of the city wall.

It was in that dark tunnel that once we, the elder brothers, and Reverend James Stuart of Cambridge Brotherhood, had come across a half-eaten calf hidden by a leopard. That dangerous animal had been shot only a few days prior to our trip, while it had taken shelter under the old culvert running between Ghiyas-ud-din's Tomb and the road to Mehrauli.

Today, no one can imagine the presence of a leopard near the fort of Tughlaqabad or around Suraj Kund. It is also strange to think how Hazrat Nizamuddin Aulia's curse on that grand citadel had come true. Till the sixties of the last century the only village inside the Tughlaq citadel was inhabited by villagers of the tribal Gujjar community. Till our young days they kept animals such as sheep or goats as livestock to earn a livelihood. When our picnic party came down to board the cars a whole group of young men and boys with a big herd of animals surrounded our cars. The fortress, towering above us, had begun to turn golden with the late afternoon sun. At that hour it was easy to imagine what Tughlaqabad must have looked like in the 14th century when, according to the traveller Ibn Batuta, all its gigantic walls used to dazzle everyone because they were painted with gold.

Our next stop was Vijay Mandal which was constructed by Mohammad Shah Tughlaq after he abandoned Tughlaqabad, where his father and his brother had been killed. The new king had decided to leave the old city and fort built

Jama Masjid, 1950

■ Clock Tower,
Chandni Chowk, 1897
(Photographer not known)

by his father. He built a new city and a palace called Jahanpanah, and Vijay Mandal, or the Victory Pavilion, appeared to be an important building. It is said that Mohammad Shah often sat on a canopy, on the top platform, to review his fighting force of both elephants and men. The nearby Begumpur Masjid was his Jami Masjid and, according to my father, a similar mosque called the Atala Masjid had been built at a town called Jaunpur in Uttar Pradesh.

Ten years after my first visit to Begumpur, I had an opportunity to visit Jaunpur and also to photograph the Atala Masjid. The similarity between these two mosques, though a long distance apart, turned out to be remarkable.

On our return drive we had to pass some of the lonely tombs near Hauz Khas, On both sides of the main road at Yusuf Sarai we saw villagers had begun to spread grains right on the road itself to dry. Such liberties could be taken with the main road to Qutb Minar because there was hardly any traffic at night. I also cannot remember the presence of any electric light. Fortunately for all of us, the railway crossing just before Safdarjung Airport was open, but a red light there warned us of an approaching aeroplane. Soon, a DC-3 aircraft, probably flying in from Kolkata, whizzed passed overhead and practically touched the rooftops of our awkwardly-shaped vintage cars. We could also see that the white dome of Safdarjung's Tomb happened to be lit with a red flood-light. It was the only Delhi monument that used to be flood-lit. One of my suggestions, ten years later, to fix lights around important historic buildings, was drastically edited out of a book that I was asked to write for the Government Tourist Department.

After dropping our two young friends and their wives at Man Nagar, now called Rabindra Nagar, we drove on towards Purana Qila to reach Mathura Road. Passing the first multi-storey blocks of flats in Delhi called Sujan Singh Park, we had to touch the northern periphery of New Delhi's exclusive Golf Club. Though we were not lucky enough to spot any animals because of the dim lights of our vintage cars, only a few days after our New Year's Eve excursion a leopard was seen loitering at night near the Golf Club scrubland. The sighting of that large feline animal was reported in a well-known English newspaper and some magazines.

However, there is a sad epilogue to add to our experience on that day. After entering Chandni Chowk at the Lahore Gate junction of Red Fort, the station wagon failed to move any further and some us had to find a tonga to reach our home at Mori Gate. As we were passing the Municipal Town Hall to enter Queen's Garden, the clock tower above us began to strike seven with its characteristic deep chimes. In less than three months this clock tower crashed down one morning and some of the unfortunate passersby were seriously injured and one or two were killed.

This seemed symbolic. The crashing of the clock tower got juxtaposed in my memory with the deepening shadows that were the inevitable result of Partition, of separating families, of bloodshed and gore, of tragedies and trauma.

Chapter 10

Charm and the City

■ Tram car in Shahjahanabad, 1951

Charm and the City

I often used trams to reach some of the interior parts of Shahjahanabad. My favourite haunt, an old haveli in Bazaar Sita Ram, fascinated me. It took me back to an era when life moved at a gentle pace

The last week of March 1951. My High School examinations were drawing to a close. Since the cold season that year was somewhat slow in its retreat I often went up to the terrace of our building not only for the warmth of the spring sunshine but also for the solitude that was necessary for my studies. Once in a while, I could not help but gaze at some of the prominent landmarks of Shahjahanabad such as the Red Fort and the tall clock tower built by the British. This rough copy of the Big Ben in London stood at the centre of Chandni Chowk. It was built in the nineteenth century, along with the first municipal town hall and the railway station. It was not only visible from our terrace, but we could also hear the deep peal booming across the old city of Shahjahanabad, particularly in the quiet hours of the night.

Around noon on that particular day, there was a sudden rumbling sound and our building shuddered for a second. What came to my mind in a flash was that earthquake-prone Delhi had been hit and that too only a day before my final examination. But since our terrace remained quite stable and the rumbling had stopped, I began to look around the city and found to my utter surprise that the old clock tower had simply vanished. It was just like a conjurer's trick, which could hardly be explained. My immediate inclination was to rush out and find out the reason behind that morning's mystery. However, the fear of my examinations kept me home.

That evening, I came to know from my home-made radio set that the prominent Ghanta Ghar, or the 'Bell Tower' of Chandni Chowk had collapsed that particular morning and killed more than one passerby. The next day, soon after my examination had ended, I boarded a tram car and reached the site of the accident.

There, I found the bronze statue of Queen Victoria outside the portico of the municipal building gazing mournfully at the ruin of that British symbol of power. Hundreds of wild pigeons fluttered around that fallen tower. The pigeons would often sit on the clock hands, not allowing it to keep proper time. This tower, as well as the Town Hall, was often attacked as a sign of protest against British rule.

Among the many reasons attributed to this accident was the constant vibration of many trams which had been rumbling across Chandni Chowk for nearly half a century. Tramcars were introduced in Shahjahanabad, and around some suburbs, Sabzi Mandi and Sadar Bazar, after electric power came to Delhi in 1903. I used them at times to move around in the old city as well as for going to Roshanara Bagh, to watch birds and buy vegetables from Sabzi Mandi. For about two annas, one could have a circular trip of the old city and some of those suburbs.

Starting from the Jama Masjid, which happened to be one of the main terminal points, trams usually moved towards Chandni Chowk after going down a road called Esplanade. Then, after taking a turn near Lahore Gate of the fort, these public transport vehicles rumbled down the Chowk and finally reached the Fatehpuri Masjid. They would go through Khari Baoli to move towards either Sadar Bazaar or Sabzi Mandi. Another route, which once again started from the Jama Masjid, took an opposite turn, and after passing through Chawri Bazaar, the wholesale paper mart of Delhi, touched Hauz Kazi and Lal Kuan to move on to the Fatehpuri Masjid through Katra Barian. It was rather sad that this pollution-free transit system, instead of being modernised, was ruthlessly taken off the streets in the late fifties or early sixties on the pretext that it obstructed traffic.

I often used trams to reach some of the interior parts of Shahjahanabad. My favourite haunt, an old haveli in Bazaar Sita Ram, fascinated me. It took me back to an era when life moved at a gentle pace. This traditional haveli belonged to Kaviraj Nibaran Chandra Bhattacharya who was one of the pioneers from Bengal and had settled down in Delhi to practice the traditional ayurvedic system of Indian medicine. He also taught regularly at Tibbia College in Karol Bagh, where Hakim Ajmal Khan had begun a medical college for teaching the unani and ayurvedic systems of medicines. Unfortunately, Nibaran Babu died early. Later this family business came to be looked after by his nephew Dr Jyotish Chandra Bhattacharya and his uncle, Pandit

Gopal Chandra Bhattacharya from Varanasi. Their traditional mansion was often my base camp in the heart of Shahjahanabad.

To reach Sita Ram Bazaar from Mori Gate, I had the choice of walking all the way, or catching a tram near the Fatehpuri Masjid at the end of Khari Baoli. Either way, I had to cross the railway line first over Dufferin Bridge and then enter an interesting old area called Phatak Habash Khan, or the Gateway of Habash Khan.

After stepping into this locality the first thing one noticed was the narrow width of all lanes and a constant tapping sound of foil beaters living in this locality. In practically every house, men of all ages, including young boys, were beating tiny silver and gold pieces into super-thin foils. These shiny foils not only made paan (betel leaf) more attractive, they were also supposed to lend some kind of aphrodisiacal properties to them.

Next came the telian or oil-crushers' locality. The courtyards of many houses here had wooden oil mills, ghani, which had a pair of blindfolded bullocks tied to each of these devices. These bullocks would go round in endless circles and the locality would be redolent with the pungent smell of crushed mustard seeds. At the end of this lane, and just before Khari Baoli, this particular lane had shops which sold all types of chemicals and dyes, including corrosive acids and toxic gases such as chlorine.

After reaching the bustling grain and spice mart of Khari Baoli, I could either board a tramcar or walk once again through another lane called Batasha Gali. Though batasha meant a particular kind of sugar meringue, many shops in this lane sold several varieties of sugar products and a whole range of pickles and preserved fruits. Many of these products, displayed on saucers and jars, had distinct flavours. After Batasha Gali I sometimes boarded a tram at the junction of two streets called Katra Bariyan and Lal Kuan or the Red Well. The old locality of Lal Kuan had remained predominantly Muslim even after Partition. When a tramcar went past clanging its warning bell, the combination of the old and the new created a unique presentation.

Among all the old houses and shops in the area, one came across many dispensaries and also two factories of the traditional unani system of medicine. Today both these establishments have not only survived but have also become big names.

■ Sari-seller on Ballimaran Street, Chandni Chowk, 1952

There was another narrow lane that branched off towards the well-known street of Ballimaran. The famous Urdu poet, Mirza Ghalib, lived here in a rented haveli belonging to Hakim Mehmud Khan. According to Ghalib's own account, every room in this house leaked like a sieve during the rainy season and many pots and pans had to be placed all around to prevent the rainwater from flooding the living rooms. Ballimaran had many other well-known hakims, or unani doctors, living there including Hakim Ajmal Khan, famous for founding Tibbia College, the first college of traditional medicine in Delhi. Ajmal Khan Road and the popular market inside Karol Bagh are named after him.

Some of the narrow lanes around Lal Kuan were inhabited by haemophrodites. They dressed as women and earned their livelihood by visiting homes which had babies or brides. Whenever I saw a group of them, I crossed over to the other side of Lal Kuan, quietly, and tried to avoid eye contact as far as possible.

Lal Kuan opened out on to a square called Hauz Kazi or Kazi Hauz, which meant the Magistrate's water reservoir. Once this particular place was considered the most spacious square of all the areas of Shahjahanabad and, in order to go into Bazaar Sita Ram, I had to get down at this place from a tram. The tram would trundle further through Chawri Bazar and finally reach the southern gate of the Jama Masjid.

After entering one of the leading Hindu localities of Old Delhi, I would come across several arched openings of lanes such as Kucha Pati Ram and Lal Darwaza, or the Red Gateway. These gateways at the beginning of nearly all lanes had solid wooden doors reinforced by iron bars and spikes. They served to prevent hostile mobs and looters from entering some of these residential areas, usually inhabited by prosperous Hindu families. Today, when I see iron gates and barricaded grills coming up in the posh new areas of Delhi I am reminded once again of those sturdy old gates of Lal Darwaza and Kucha Pati Ram.

The ancestral house of the Bhattacharya family in Bazaar Sita Ram was a typical example of a haveli built during the resettlement of the old city in the latter half of the nineteenth century. The main entrance to such a traditional building was through an archway and a narrow passage leading to a central courtyard. Around this courtyard were usually a number of rooms with colonnades which, at times, were used for either business or as a service area for cooking meals and even for keeping cows. Generally, living areas including all bedrooms were usually on upper floors, which often rose up to many more than the two storeys allowed by the British rulers. All these rooms opened inward to a running balcony around the central courtyard. Only a limited view of the sky was possible from these inward-opening doors and windows. Often these views too were barred with solid iron grills and thick wire mesh to keep out the marauding monkeys and many flocks of blue pigeons which were always fluttering about in the old city, looking for places to roost.

Most of the people who lived in these traditional houses belonged to a joint family known till today, for the purpose of income tax, as Hindu Undivided Family.

More often than not, the overall control of the entire family, including the ancestral residential house, was bestowed on the seniormost patriarch in that family. All married members usually had a room or two allotted to them according to their ranks and all others, except for the infant children, slept in large rooms used like dormitories. These large bedrooms were always strictly segregated according to sex and were monitored by a widowed mother or an aunt.

■ Chess-players at a haveli in Bazaar Sita Ram, 1953

Since men and even boys spent most of their waking hours outside to earn a living, or for studies, this lack of privacy hardly created a problem in the daily routine of these joint families. The only other facilities, that were commonly used, were bathrooms as well as toilets. Those were often on the topmost roof, or in a dark and rather damp corner next to the staircase. As for meals, everyone was supposed to take his or her daily meal from the common kitchen usually located on the ground floor and managed by more than one cook.

Moving on to the main source of entertainment, there were one or two radio sets operating from rooms occupied by the most affluent members of the joint family. Women had little opportunity for entertainment, as they were busy attending to their children and daily religious rituals. The preparation of condiments and pickles, which were always put on the roof for maturing and drying, provided them fresh air and an opportunity to gossip about their locality across many rooftops of the old city.

However, young men and boys had rather limited access to the rooftops and were allowed only in certain seasons to fly kites. At times, after giving proper notice to clear the floor, they could also indulge in what was popularly called Kabutar Bazi, or pigeon tournament. This traditional form of entertainment dating to the Mughal times could often be seen near our house.

The men living in these large families usually cleared their business spaces on the ground floor in the evenings and assembled here for gossiping or for playing some traditional games such as Shatranj and Pachisi.

While working on a photo-feature called 'Delhi, Old and New', I had the fortunate experience of visiting an old haveli at Lal Darwaza, where the men were very fond of playing chess in their baithak or the sitting room. The scene there resembled many of the shots that could be seen decades later in Satyajit Ray's film, *Shatranj-ke-Khilari*.

My experience at an old house in Neel-ka-Katra in Chandni Chowk is difficult to forget. This narrow lane, named as the mart of old vegetable indigo dye, was never more than ten to twelve feet wide and yet all houses on both the sides were so high that sunlight hardly reached the ground. Most of the shops here sold cloth pieces cut into odd sizes. Some of the richest Hindu merchants such as Lala Chunna Mal had their havelis right at a corner of this cramped lane.

One winter evening towards the end of 1951, I acted as a pathfinder to a French journalist, who had come to meet my father after reading his just-published autobiography. This person wanted to visit someone whose business address was located at Katra Neel. After entering a traditional haveli through a stone archway, we came upon a gloomy courtyard, where a meal was being cooked on a fire fuelled with wood. We had to wait for some minutes while our names were taken up to one of the masters of that traditional house. All of a sudden we were rather startled to hear the famous opening bars of Beethoven's Fifth Symphony.

When we were taken upstairs to a modern drawing-room we found that the gentleman we had come to meet was listening to the classic symphony on a radiogram fitted with facilities for playing long-playing discs. Today, in this age of media explosion, such an occurrence can be shrugged off easily, but in the early fifties to hear that famous symphony in a traditional haveli at Katra Neel was a unique experience.

Pranab Guha was about to leave Delhi, along with his wife, after being selected for the prestigious Indian Foreign Service. Apart from losing a wonderful friend, Pranab Babu's departure meant that his camera would no longer be available for my project of photographing the historic buildings of Delhi.

To make most of the time available to me, I set off one evening for the Jama Masjid, when wonderful monsoon clouds were seen over Delhi. The best view that I could find of the Jama Masjid was from Edward Park. That was where the grand Akbarabadi Masjid had stood. Later, that mosque got demolished in the clearing-up operation around the Red Fort. However, an old photograph taken by an English photographer called Beato in 1858 from the top of the Jama Masjid clearly shows the presence of this particular mosque.

My picture of the Jama Masjid of Shahjahanabad was taken as a silhouette against the evening sky, and in the foreground there were tall palm trees, which had been planted around an equestrian statue of King Edward the VII.

Within a couple of weeks, I was back at the same spot inside Edward Park when I found that the familiar statues of Nicholson and Taylor had just disappeared overnight from the parks outside Mori Gate. I wanted to photograph the only equestrian statue of a British king in Delhi. Though the statue of King Edward on horseback had been considered rather ugly by the eminent art critic Charles Fabri, my picture was commended as remarkable by that well-known art lover.

Within a short time I joined Hindu College. Shanti Bhattacharya, a cousin of Khokada who had passed the final examination along with me, joined the old Delhi College outside Ajmere Gate, which functioned at that time from a Mughal building, which had an old mosque and also Ghazi-ud-Din's tomb.

My father's famous book *The Autobiography of an Unknown Indian* was published after I joined college and almost overnight he became a celebrity. But just after one year he was told to retire quite abruptly and he hardly got any retirement benefits. So while I began to get some of my work published in newspapers and an illustrated magazine, sometimes I had to act as a guide to some of my father's foreign readers, who were curious about Shahjahanabad.

One autumn morning in 1952, I accompanied an English lady to Bazaar Sita Ram to see the private Durga Puja festival at the Bhattacharyas' haveli. From Mori Gate we walked all through the usual old route to Sita Ram Bazaar and, in spite of the congestion and the odd remarks by local people, including a few eunuchs, the lady was thrilled. She was received with great warmth by all the women of Khokada's family. After seeing the ritual conducted by Gopal Mama himself, the lady took an active part in offering the anjali, an offering of flowers. Later she ate the home-made prasad of Indian sweets and fruits with great reverence and delight.

After attending the Durga Puja celebration at Bazaar Sita Ram, we resumed our walk towards Turkman Gate. My European companion was amazed to see more than one sturdy bull roaming around the vegetable stalls of that Hindu locality. After we reached the Tughlaq mosque of Kalan, built by Emperor Feroz Shah, the ethnic character of this old locality changed rapidly to fit its original name, which was Kucha Syed Qasim Khan.

The people of this locality were predominantly Muslim and the presence of many cows and bulls seen at Sita Ram Bazaar had been replaced by a number of goats, chewing bunches of leaves. Instead of only vegetables, people here were selling eggs and chicken and many were seen jostling in the narrow confines of that old locality. The Kalan Masjid remained an oasis of tranquility. Standing at the high gate of Kalan Masjid, one could get an impressive view of the Jama Masjid as well as the cityscape. After coming out of Turkman Gate, we had to cross the rubble of the old Mughal walls along with scores of houses more than centuries old. The remaining portion of the old city wall around Turkman Gate was demolished long ago to give way to the commercial buildings of Asaf Ali Road. The demolition of the old houses near Turkman Gate, as late as 1976, created a major political upheaval in Delhi.

After coming out of Shahjahanabad at Turkman Gate, where the oldest slaughterhouse of Delhi was still in use, we began to walk across the main Ram Lila Ground at the southern limit of the old city. That open ground, stretching from Ajmere Gate to Delhi Gate, was really green, as was Lutyens' New Delhi. From there we hired a tonga. My reward for conducting that pioneering walk was an unexpected but splendid lunch at Wenger's.

Chapter 11

With a Camera in Lutyens' Delhi

Rashtrapati Bhawan, 1953

With a Camera in Lutyens' Delhi

After getting down to work on the feature, 'Acropolis of Delhi', I purchased an old plate camera from a small photo shop, owned by a refugee family from Lahore. The cost of that Zeiss camera was about fifty rupees

April 1953. A Sunday morning; the sky over New Delhi is bright and blue. It was an ideal day for taking outdoor pictures. Standing at the top of the Samrat Yantra of Jantar Mantar, I had a wide panoramic view of the President's House along with the twin blocks of Central Secretariat and Parliament House. Around me there was not a single multi-storeyed building, and the War Memorial Arch, or India Gate as it is called now, was the only man-made structure visible above the tree-line. I had climbed that observatory triangle, built by Raja Jai Singh of Jaipur, to take a photograph of the New Delhi skyline to illustrate an article, 'The Acroplis of Delhi: An Architectural Trio'.

Today this expression, 'Acropolis of Delhi', originally used by Sir Herbert Baker, has become a cliché. Yet way back in 1953, when I was struggling hard to prepare this illustrated feature on New Delhi, there were hardly any books or other written material readily available on New Delhi. After searching through many of the bookshops at Connaught Place, I could trace an important biography of Sir Edwin Lutyens, along with the three other bulky volumes on New Delhi's architecture, published in London. But as it was impossible to buy those costly volumes. I had to take the help of our kind and erudite friend OK Ghosh for going through them at the Central Secretariat Library. Among other details it was rather exciting to find that Rashtrapati Bhawan was meant to resemble Versailles in France and the trio of the important buildings on Raisina Hill were to look like the Acropolis in Athens. That was how the particular title for my article came to be chosen.

For more than two decades after New Delhi was inaugurated in 1931, there were hardly any articles or illustrated features about the new capital. The first paragraph of my article read: "New Delhi has an architectural history of great human, political and artistic interest. But very little attention is paid to it. One reason for this neglect is the existence of the older Islamic monuments, which not only overshadow the creations of our times, but also allows the snobbish to raise their eyebrows at them. There may also be a deeper nationalist factor. Every nationalist leader, including Mahatma Gandhi, deplored the expenditure on this architectural pile as a colossal waste of money."

To overcome such objections by nationalist leaders, Lutyens tried to get Pandit Motilal Nehru, the father of Pandit Nehru and also a great nationalist leader, interested in the project of building New Delhi. However, we have no evidence that Motilal Nehru did anything substantial for Lutyens. The financial implications created a sense of antipathy towards New Delhi in many Indian leaders. A good deal of that antipathy was still in evidence in the capital after five years of independence from British rule.

My first article, 'Acropolis of Delhi', was published on August 2, 1953. At the beginning of this article I mentioned that the three imperial buildings of Lutyens and Baker were the only distinctive examples of modern architecture in Delhi. Without them the capital of free India was running the risk of becoming a mere encampment of hutments that had sprung up all over New Delhi at the time of World War II and Partition.

The question of a suitable site for this new capital became important after the area near Coronation Pillar, where the Delhi Durbar of 1911 was held, was given up. The land around the Coronation Pillar was swampy and liable to flooding. In my boyhood days we often saw black bucks and neelgai grazing there. At present the site around the Coronation Pillar is a reposing ground for many British statues that once decorated all parts of Delhi.

There were many conflicting views regarding a suitable location for the new capital and among other possibilities even Yamuna Paar, or the left bank of the river, received serious consideration. Finally, the site around Raisina Hill was chosen almost by accident after abandoning another site on nearby Malcha Hill. Lord Hardinge wrote that he, accompanied by Lord Hailey, the then Chief Commissioner of Delhi, had galloped up Raisina Hill to take a look. From that high point, the Viceroy had a wonderful view of the entire countryside along with many of the old monuments and the

Yamuna flowing down. This was the site that was finally selected for the Viceroy's House as well as for the two blocks of the Secretariat. Of course, the chief architect Edwin Lutyens and his co-designer Herbert Baker had already seen Raisina Hill while riding an elephant and were taken up with its many possibilities.

A twin-lens reflex camera, which Pranab Guha had so kindly allowed me to use, was ideal for the type of work I was hoping to do. But he had been posted far away to Singapore and to afford a camera like a Rolleiflex or even a Rolleicord was almost next to impossible.

A few months earlier, while working on a feature called 'Delhi – Old & New', I had managed to buy a Voightlander folding camera, Perkeo, from a photo studio at Regal Building. The owner, BK Dilwali, was kind enough to give me a camera at a throwaway price of less than two hundred rupees. That camera proved to be rather lucky for me. On the same day after buying it, I managed to get a real unusual shot of Connaught Place. The picture showed a traditionally dressed pot-seller and a couple of donkeys against the gleaming arcades of Connaught Place. That uncommon picture became an immediate success. After getting down to work on the feature, 'Acropolis of Delhi', I purchased an old plate camera from a small photo shop, owned by a refugee family from Lahore. The cost of that Zeiss camera was about fifty rupees. I had a wooden tripod rebuilt from scrap.

The narrow space around the sundial on top of the highest structure of Jantar Mantar was not enough to operate a cumbersome plate-camera on a tripod. After struggling with the focus and exposure settings for more than half-an-hour I managed to expose a single photographic plate. This aged and rather fragile glass plate has stood the test of time well and still depicts a unique view of the New Delhi skyline. Today, it is neither possible to go up on Samrat Yantra easily, nor will the view be so open and serene.

After coming down from that high viewpoint at Jantar Mantar, I walked along the unique cycle path on Parliament Street. As it was a Sunday, it was almost deserted, and served well as a shaded footpath. The entire area around Parliament House at that time was remarkably open and free. The only signs of restrictions were for bullock carts, which used to create havoc on Delhi roads with their steel-rimmed wheels. Less than a hundred yards from this signpost, and right under one of the blocks of Central Secretariat, I witnessed and

■ South Block, Central Secretariat, 1953

also photographed a rare scene involving two bullock carts.

I had set up my large plate camera on a tripod near the Boat Club, and while my head was under a black cloth for focusing I suddenly saw an upside-down view of two bullock carts moving across the glass screen of my plate camera. The eternal Indian bullock carts looked almost surrealistic against the majestic Secretariat. Abandoning my slow camera on a tripod I ran across to grab that unusual shot of Herbert Baker's architecture with my Perkeo always ready for a decisive shot.

After that exciting shot, it was positively boring to concentrate on the controversial gradient between the two Secretariat buildings which I was trying to illustrate. It was Baker who was responsible for this steep gradient which obliterates the view of the President's house. As soon as it had been decided to place the Secretariat on Raisina Hill and move the Viceroy's House 400 yards to the west, Lutyens had serious misgivings about the visibility of the house designed by him. He tried to persuade his friend to revise the slope. But Baker realised what an advantage it would be to have a wide open square between the two Secretariat buildings and stuck to the crucial agreement signed by the two principal designers of New Delhi. Lutyens in absolute fury took the matter to King George V. But Lord Chelmsford, who had become the Viceroy by that time, could not take cognisance of the privately expressed view of a constitutional monarch and not the government. Lutyens never forgave Baker for letting him down after being a friend of long standing and was never reconciled to this blunder.

Since I could not manage to take a photograph of that gradient, which highlighted the problem in an adequate way, I had to concentrate on the styles of architecture and, particularly, on the many arches and domes. There were practically no restrictions those days to walk around in those corridors of power. I managed to get an unusual shot of the South Block, from a wrought iron gateway of the North Block. The guard standing at that gateway was helpful in adjusting that massive gate at an angle suitable for photography.

Not only did that photograph become the lead picture for my feature, but the magazine editor, an Englishman and a professional to the core, readily agreed to my proposal for two more illustrated features on Lutyens' New Delhi.

It was at that point in time that I had to face a major hurdle for photographing the President's House. In 1949, when some of the main halls of Rashtrapati Bhawan were thrown open as the National Museum, I could photograph the Durbar Hall easily as well as the main façade with many Imperial lions. But by 1953 the residence of the President had become more exclusive and so I decided to write a polite letter to the Military Secretary requesting permission to photograph Rashtrapati Bhawan. To my great surprise, the permission arrived within three days and allowed me to photograph the President's House from the various angles required to illustrate the articles on the architecture of New Delhi.

Besides laying down some principles of architectural styles, Lord Hardinge had also recommended as models some of the Indian buildings he had seen and admired. Among them, the Hindola Mahal at Mandu particularly took his fancy. He was fascinated by the pointed arch of Islamic architecture. Thus, Lutyens found it necessary to study Mughal and Hindu monuments to decide if they could provide a starting-point for his buildings.

Baker, however, did not have much difficulty in following this line. He told Lutyens that in a new political capital the politician's standpoint must be recognised. He also advised Lutyens that the architects should not conflict with Indian sentiment, while the main buildings of New Delhi followed the general Renaissance style. The question of pointed or round arches was also discussed threadbare.

Lutyens was ready to integrate into his design some of the basic shapes and motifs of Indian architecture. He fancied the shape of stupas and their railings. He also included some features that the Mughals had employed to counteract the fierce effect of the Indian sunlight. According to him, the Mughals had protected colours by using red sandstone. The outline and the main form of a Mughal building was taken care of by providing deep cornices to cast sharp shadows to reduce the blurring effect of the bright sunshine. Lutyens had hit upon these two optical effects with a good deal of success and in some of my photographs these points were highlighted for the first time.

In another article, 'Where India's President Lives', I highlighted the sad fact that there was, at that time, a national lack of consciousness. This particular article, with a large four-column picture of the President's House with the Jaipur column in the foreground, began like this: "The

Rashtrapati Bhawan, Republic Day, 1956

transformation of the seat of the British Viceroy of India into the residence of the President of the Indian Republic is a great romance of history. It is also one of its greatest dramas. Thus it appears odd that nothing is being done to bring home this change by making the nation proud of its presidential mansion. The practice of throwing the Mughal Gardens open to the public for a few weeks in the cold season dates back to British times. The only innovation since Independence is the changed name. Viceroy's House has now become Rashtrapati Bhawan."

Though all the three illustrated articles on Lutyens' New Delhi were well received by eminent people such as Khushwant Singh and Som Nath Chib, the first Director-General of Tourism, I had to curtail my photojournalism activities for almost two years because of the pressure of studies for a B.Sc. Honours degree. But before going into that unique area of Delhi devoted to higher studies, it may be appropriate to describe a rare experience which I had in 1955, to photograph Lutyens' New Delhi from an aeroplane. The actual assignment given to me was to cover a group of public school students taking a joy-ride over New Delhi. I literally grabbed that opportunity not only to fly for the first time in an aeroplane, but also to photograph New Delhi with a roll of 35 mm colour film and use a Leica camera. That camera was lent to me by one of my uncles, a reputed doctor from Kolkata, who happened to be an enthusiastic amateur photographer.

We took off from Safdarjung Airport in a Dakota, or DC-3, which had just arrived from Srinagar in Kashmir. After crossing the river near the Humayun's Tomb, the plane flew towards Old Delhi and while passing over the Purana Qila we had a wonderful view of the Central Vista with the President's House and the two Secretariat buildings on Raisina Hill gleaming in the horizon. Then, after flying for a few minutes over the old city including the Jama Masjid and the Red Fort, our pilot, a tall Sikh gentleman, took a turn towards Connaught Place where the gulmohur trees looked glorious with their bright orange blooms.

Then we flew over Birla Mandir, the most prominent Hindu temple of New Delhi. The main roads and avenues looked symmetrical and yet had interesting vistas. Photographing New Delhi from the air was an experience that I could never repeat. Sadly, all those precious slides simply vanished from my collection as well as from New Delhi. These are the shadows that add gloom to one's thoughts and darken even the happiest of memories.

Chapter 12

A New Focus

Bus stop near Delhi University, 1955

A New Focus

Looking at the familiar skyline of New Delhi and thinking about my future I realised that this particular phase of my life, stretching for nearly five years since my New Year's resolution taken on Vijay Mandal, was about to be over

At the start of 1955, when my B.Sc. Honours examination was approaching, I realised that it was not possible to pursue my studies along with my interest in photojournalism.

Though I had enrolled as a student of Hindu College, our science classes were conducted at the science faculty building next to the old Viceregal Lodge. The first building of the University of Delhi was a sprawling white bungalow that, after housing no less than four Viceroys, Hardinge, Chemsford, Reading and Irwin, has also housed the Vice Chancellor's office.

The main library of the University, too, was in a huge hall, which served as the ballroom till 1932. It was here that Lord Louis Mountbatten had proposed to Edwina Ashley. A plaque in the Registrar's office announces this event in the life of the last Viceroy.

After taking over as the Vice Chancellor of Delhi University, Sir Maurice Gwyer had visualised that this large palace of an imperial bungalow, along with the vast empty area beyond the Ridge of Delhi, would be an ideal conclave of higher studies. Like the university towns of Oxford and Cambridge, important colleges functioning in Delhi were allotted land around the main university building. St. Stephen's College was the first to move into this exclusive University area beyond Delhi's picturesque Ridge. This college building was designed by a British architect called Blomefield. He set the trend of using exposed brick in all colleges as well as the faculty buildings of the University.

When I joined Hindu College it had only its hostel and principal's residence located right across St. Stephen's campus. The main Hindu College building, after lying unfinished for nearly a decade, was completed, and the college moved from Skinner's old bungalow in the autumn of 1953. After this move, we had less distance to commute between our University and college classes. But somehow many of us sadly missed those old and rather musty classrooms and the rotunda of an assembly hall.

Among the other notable colleges and institutions of higher learning that functioned around the University campus at that time was Miranda House for Women and the elite Gwyer Hall for post-graduate students and research scholars. These research scholars sometimes took our under-graduate practical classes. Some of them became good friends. Occasionally, when some of us were invited for lunch at this prestigious institution, we felt honoured and enjoyed the academic atmosphere long before I went to England for my studies in 1971.

The new Arts Faculty building along with the Convocation Hall had also just been completed. We often rushed to that new hall to hear eminent scientists and Nobel laureates such as Linus Pauling or Irene Curie. There was another outstanding institution of Delhi University, the Delhi School of Economics. This important institution had started functioning at that time under the able leadership of Dr VKRV Rao. The future Nobel laureate from India, Professor Amartya Sen, could often be seen here.

The general atmosphere of my student days at the University campus was rather relaxed and trouble-free. Party politics could hardly raise its ugly head among the students of Delhi University. We science students always had a busy schedule, and, if during a rare free period we could go down to the bustling and noisy coffee house, we used to consider ourselves lucky. That University coffee house was always a lively place and provided an interesting meeting-place for students of different colleges, particularly of nearby Miranda House.

Another occasion when all the students of the Delhi University had a good time was after the winter recess, when the inter-college cricket match was held. This match was usually played at the large cricket ground in front of the Vice Chancellor's office. More often than not, the St. Stephen's and Hindu College teams were the main contenders at the final match, which was played like a full-fledged test match for five days. Here, all round the cricket field, the Miranda girls usually cheered the St. Stephen's team, while some of the girls from Indraprastha, who were studying science,

■ Left to right: Pandit Nehru, Prince Philip, Dr Radhakrishnan and Dr VKRV Rao at a convocation in Delhi University, 1959

supported the Hindu team in a rather subdued manner. Among our group of close friends and fellow students, there were two boys from Hindu College, three girls from Miranda House and one from Indraprastha College. This group of ours was rather atypical at that time, because we belonged to colleges that were considered distinctly different in their outlook and educational values.

The other channels of entertainment during our college days were rather limited, and the idea of going to see a film in a group, and certainly not as a couple, was difficult if not impossible. However, a few weeks before our final examination we all decided to have a good parting celebration and went to see a romantic film, *Three Coins In The Fountain* filmed in Rome, a city which was remarkable in its similarity with the historic city of Delhi.

At last in the late autumn of 1955 and after a gap of nearly six months following our exams, my group of friends assembled once again

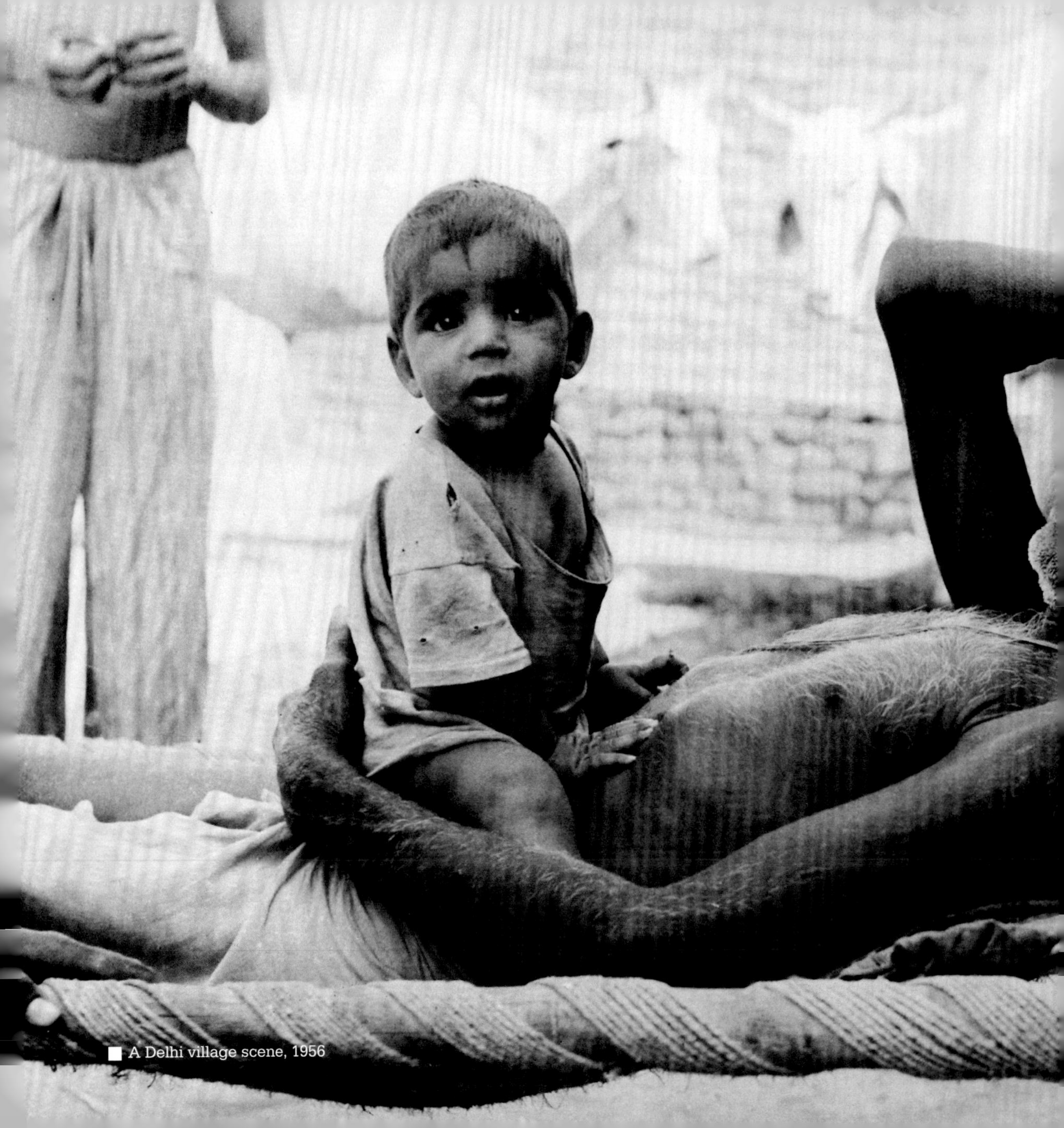

A Delhi village scene, 1956

at the portico of the old Viceroy's House. The occasion was the annual convocation scheduled on that day. All of us had to wear a formal black gown and also a mortar-board to receive our degrees with a solemn bow to the Vice Chancellor.

A few weeks later my close friend and class mate Nimai Majumdar and I went down to the Central Vista to see the Russian President, Bulganin and Communist Party chief, Kruschev, the de facto ruler, arrive in New Delhi. They drove all the way from Palam Airport in an open light blue Packard accompanied by Pandit Nehru.

The Russian leaders were given a warm welcome by a huge crowd from all over Delhi, and the surrounding states, too. These leaders waved to all those gathered along the route that stretched right up to one of the main gates of Rashtrapati Bhawan.

This kind of free and spontaneous reception to foreign and national leaders by an Indian crowd became a typical feature of New Delhi those days. After an interval of four years once again such scenes were repeated by the Delhi crowd at the state arrival of President Eisenhower, the first President of the United States to visit India.

On our way back, Nimai and I decided to walk down to Connaught Place for a cup of coffee. From the Boat Club lawn we noticed that two huge blocks of office buildings, Udyog and Krishi Bhawan, had been built on both sides of Central Vista. Thus the original concept of Lutyens and Baker, to have an open view from all points of King's Way and Central Vista, had vanished for good.

As chance would have it, within less than a year I was once again looking at the familiar skyline on Raisina Hill from one of the top-floor windows of the newly completed Krishi Bhawan building. I, along with three other young photographers, who had been shortlisted for a photographer's post, were anxiously waiting for the final result after a tough interview. Looking at the familiar skyline of New Delhi and thinking about my future I realised that this particular phase of my life, stretching for nearly five years since my New Year's resolution taken on Vijay Mandal, was about to be over.

In those years many historical sites such as Humayun's Tomb and Purana Qila, which had become camps for the refugees from West Pakistan, were restored once again to their original glory. Refugee settlements such as Shakti Nagar, Lajpat Nagar, Gandhi Nagar and Patel Nagar had come up in rapid succession. Also, swampy or arid lands around Delhi were transformed into thriving colonies such as Model Town, Sunder Nagar and Greater Kailash. Multi-storeyed office blocks had come up in rapid succession and housed many of the expanding ministries of independent India.

As for myself, I did manage to graduate with a science degree and had earned a bit as a freelance photojournalist too. But the money was definitely not enough to meet the demand of a family in want, and it became imperative for me to find a job with a regular salary and some security. So there I was sitting in one of the rooms of Krishi Bhawan along with the three other young men who had chosen photography as their profession. I had crossed the first barrier of a tough interview conducted by some of the high officials of the agriculture ministry, including an Indian Civil Service officer with a consuming interest in the art and cultural life of Delhi.

However, after an improvised lunch of South Indian snacks and coffee, all four of us were bundled into a Jeep and asked to proceed to the village of Mahipalpur and prepare a photo-feature on rural activities. That village was considered a progressive one. On that warm

■ Skinner's Bungalow, the remains of Hindu College, 2001

and humid afternoon in the month of early September, we rushed around with our cameras. This village, which was only a few miles from Qutb Minar, is completely unrecognisable today. We vied with one another to create the best photo-feature out of the usual rural scenes – women fetching water from the common well and sturdy men working in the field with their equally sturdy bullocks. Village elders with large turbans on their heads, smoking hookahs at the village meeting-place called the chaupal, turned out to be a subject that none of us could resist. Though I did not get that job because of many reasons other than the required skill in photography, it was a valuable experience to work for the first time in a village. Later, some of those rural pictures were published in well-known foreign as well as Indian newspapers.

This village of Mahipalpur had remained totally rustic for many centuries, like many other villages around Delhi. Then in a time-span of less than two decades, it leapt into the modern Delhi of the 20th century. This is a typical example among rural pockets of Delhi. Yet one early morning of summer 1952, when I was learning to drive a car, using the old Austin, I came across a pair of hyenas trotting along the narrow road connecting Mahipalpur with Mehrauli. These animals were coming from the direction of an old tomb, Sultan Ghari, which was only a stone's throw from Mahipalpur.

This tomb was built like a small fortress. Its numerous domes were conical in shape, like the early domes of Quwwat-ul-Islam next to Qutb Minar. It is one of the earliest tombs built in Delhi, in 1229, on the last resting place of the eldest son of the Sultan Iltutmish.

On that day of my practical test for a job, I could not resist the temptation of walking across to those ruins. I was rewarded with a photograph of a peacock with a magnificent long tail strutting ahead of a bevy of five peahens. Today such a scene in Mahipalpur, around the new area of Vasant Kunj, would be impossible.

On our return trip to Krishi Bhawan well after sunset, we had to drive past the dark and solitary form of the Jamali Kamali Masjid standing against a bare landscape. Also at some distance beyond a tomb, which was once Sir Thomas Metcalf's summerhouse called Dilkusha, the tall silhouette of Qutb Minar appeared as a lone sentinel guarding all the historical relics, including Lalkot, the ruins of the Hindu qila. Though the evening was still young, many cicadas had already started their monotonous chants among the scrublands around Mehrauli. From the not-so-distant village of Sultanpur long drawn-out howls of village dogs created a sense of loneliness.

A few weeks later, after torrential rains, there was a severe earthquake which left a wide crack in the new building of the Reserve Bank of India on Parliament Street. It was then that some of the rare volumes from my father's library fell on a divan where I was sleeping. I had just completed an article: 'The Stones of Delhi'. It got published in a tourist supplement of a leading English paper from Kolkata and Delhi. This photo-feature on Delhi was my last effort on this subject. In it I had written: "Delhi is a real museum of Indo-Islamic architecture. Some of its monuments– the Qutb Minar, Red Fort, Jama Masjid, to mention only three – are famous throughout India, if not the world, and their popularity is only too evident in the large number of sightseers, both Indian and foreign, who come to see them. But what is not so well known is the fact the nowhere else in India is the history of Muslim architecture in this country so fully illustrated, and within a radius of only a few miles.

"Beginning with the Quwwat-ul-Islam mosque in the Qutb enclosure and ending with the mosque in Qudsia Bagh and the tomb of Safdarjang, Delhi offers an uninterrupted series of buildings of every style and covering every phase of the city's history. Even examples of ancient Indian architecture, like the two Ashoka Pillars along with the famous Iron Pillar, can be seen here; besides, a large number of Hindu temple columns form part of the mosque at the foot of the Minar.

"A new phase of Indo-Islamic architecture began with the tomb of Humayun, but the Purana Qila, or the Old Fort on Mathura Road which was built by Sher Shah Suri, is the last important monument in the Pathan style in Delhi. Humayun's Tomb is probably the most beautiful and impressive building in Delhi, and as magnificent as the Taj in its own way.

"The great Jama Masjid of Delhi is one of the finest examples of great mosques in this world, and in the overall design a magnificent example of Moghul architecture. This mosque is seen at its best from the outside, but such is its tragic fate today that it cannot be seen from a single point without many tin sheds and squalid buildings spoiling the view. With the Jama Masjid the great tradition of building in Delhi comes to a close. The later buildings like the Moti Masjid, the Tomb of Safdarjung and Fatehpuri Masjid are the main monuments, which mark the stages of the decline of Mughal architecture in India."

And, in concluding, I summed up: "The stones of Delhi tell two stories equally well – one of architecture and the other the human tale, of the rise and fall of empires." If only the stones could speak, there would be many more enchanting tales for us to hear; stories and anecdotes that would recreate a Delhi of long ago. Where the lengthening shadows play on our imagination; where history and legend meet the present day.

Chapter 13

Close-up

An exhibition at Pragati Maidan, 1956

Close-up

We had a stream of literary celebrities and diplomats visiting our modest flat at Mori Gate. At times it was rather odd to see more than one luxury car – the French Ambassador's Jaguar, the Canadian High Commissioner's Cadillac, a Rolls Royce from the British High Commission – regularly parked before our house

The article 'Stones of Delhi' was published in the second week of December 1956. And though I was getting my features published regularly, the honorarium received vanished within a few days. With one brother studying in England, and the youngest still to cross the hurdle of entering a college, it was extremely tough on my mother to manage the financial burden of our family. So, to extend the field of my activities in photography and to earn some cash, I began to visit the Old Secretariat building, which was within walking distance from our house.

When at the Durbar of 1911 King George V announced that Delhi would once again become the capital city, the twin-towered Old Secretariat was built in a hurry. It served as the Secretariat and Legislative Assembly before the New Delhi buildings got completed in 1932. After August 15, 1947, a large wing of this sprawling old building was turned into the Publications Division, under the Ministry of Information and Broadcasting. This division had a good photography department as well as an extensive photo library. Both these units were always busy with demands for photographs meant for all kinds of publications.

Right from my student days I used to meet T Kasinath, the chief photo editor, to take his advice on all aspects of photography. After completing my studies, my visits to him became more frequent. The Publications Division was always on the look-out for good photographs and paid well for pictures selected for government magazines and books. One such magazine, *The March Of India*, had often published my features on Delhi, Chandigarh and Jaipur. While on a visit to the Old Secretariat, I came to know that Khushwant Singh had just taken over the editorship of a new periodical called *Yojana*, meant for publicising the Five-Year Plan. As an editor he was looking for contributions that would give a different look to that new magazine.

I knew Khushwant Singh well during his All India Radio days, when I seemed to have impressed him with my precocious ability to identify vintage wines. Since Khushwantji's office was also located at Old Secretariat, I lost no time in seeking an appointment. He responded rather kindly to my suggestions for two features and even offered to lend me his own Rolleiflex camera. That twin-lens reflex camera at that time was a dream equipment for a photojournalist and was the choice of veterans such as Margaret Bourke-White.

One of the subjects agreed upon was the newly-built New Delhi station and the air-conditioned Deluxe Express, which had just begun its run between Delhi and Kolkata. This superfast train was the precursor of the Rajdhani Express.

Today, with 258 trains, and more than 300,000 passengers passing, on an average, through New Delhi station alone, it is difficult to imagine that one of my pictures, of the main foyer of this station, shows less than a dozen persons. The standard of cleanliness at that new station would be difficult, if not impossible, to imagine after almost 50 years. This was an exciting assignment for me. For the first time I had an opportunity to use a flash gun and I went on enthusiastically popping flash bulbs at various trains and at all types of steam engines.

The area outside the new building of the New Delhi station was still ruled by a brood of tonga wallahs. There were very few three-wheelers and a couple of taxis, which often stood aloof in their stands and seldom got mixed up with any other animal or mechanical vehicle for hire.

The theme of another feature for *Yojana* was an international UNESCO conference scheduled to be held at the newly-constructed Vigyan Bhawan. With the coming up of Vigyan Bhawan, off the Central Vista, New Delhi got, for the first time, an auditorium and conference rooms with the latest sound equipment and superb acoustics. I still remember watching the final plenary session from a translator's booth.

The address of Prime Minister Jawaharlal Nehru to that august international assembly impressed me considerably, as did his elegant costume with his customary red rose pinned to a cream achkan.

A few years later it was in the same hall of Vigyan Bhawan that I heard for the first time the famous Vienna Philharmonic Orchestra with Herbert von Karajan conducting it. It was a thrill not only to hear the famous opening bars of Beethoven's Fifth Symphony but also to find among a large Delhi audience, Pandit Nehru and his elegant daughter, the future Prime Minister of India, Indira Gandhi.

Before Vigyan Bhawan was built, the auditorium of National Physical Laboratory was the only other hall where western classical music recitals were held in Delhi. That hall, located at the other side of New Delhi's Ridge, was the venue for recitals given by great musicians such as Yehudi Menuhin and Isaac Stern. Here, too, we would often see Pandit Nehru accompanied by Indira Gandhi listening intently to the classics of Mozart, Beethoven and even the modern compositions of Bela Bartok. Those concerts, which were often performed late at night, had an aura of great elegance, with no presence of obvious security personnel or measures.

Almost fifty years later, I recall with certain nostalgia the civilised and almost relaxed atmosphere in which those concerts and art exhibitions took place. Whether in Vigyan

Indrani Rehman, 1957

Dhanraj Bhagat at work, 1958

Bhawan, Sapru House, or some of the varied art exhibitions held at AIFACS halls, security personnel were always there, with dignitaries such as President Rajendra Prasad and later Dr Radhakrishnan.

When we came to Delhi in the early forties, neither the Old nor New Delhi had an art exhibition hall or an auditorium worthy of the capital city. The usual venues for art exhibitions were either the New Delhi Town Hall, or, after 1946, the abandoned wartime church on Parliament Street. This temporary church building next to Broadcasting House was taken over by the All India Fine Arts & Crafts Society, known as AIFACS. As for museums worthy of India's capital, the Governor-General's House was the chosen venue till 1950 and even there anyone could walk right up to the main Durbar Hall with a camera. It was here that I first saw the beautiful Didarganj Yakshi, and also the standing Buddha statue from Sarnath.

At Regal Theatre in Connaught Place I first saw the famous dancer Uday Shankar and his troupe and some Shakespearean plays performed by Geoffrey Kendall and his well-known company. Music performances were usually held on a rather modest scale and the venue was the tiny Massey Hall of YMCA on Jai Singh Road.

Today, at the turn of this century, this hall with so many memories is lying a half-demolished ruin. Yet, once the same hall resounded with the music of Pandit Ravi Shankar, sarod player Ali Akbar Khan and the famous violinist Mehli Mehta, the father of conductor Zubin Mehta.

One of the first public halls that opened in New Delhi was the auditorium on the top floor of Sapru House on Barakhamba Road. Sapru House was the first cultural centre near Mandi House, which now with all the three academies and no less than four auditoria and art centres, has become one of the richest cultural complexes of New Delhi. However, way back in 1956, the best art and theatre centre was at the AIFACS building.

For almost a year I was a regular visitor to the new AIFACS building not only for the art and photographic exhibitions, but also to browse through the rich collection of books and magazines at the British Council library. One evening towards the end of 1956, I ran across the secretary of AIFACS, a portly Bengali painter of modest fame, with great organising skills. I knew him well since my boyhood days. He asked me in his typical blunt way, if I would be interested in a part-time job as photographer at AIFACS.

That art society was about to organise the third salon of international art and needed someone to handle the photographic publicity of that important exhibition. I lost no time in accepting the offer. Those few months of work there not only gave me a little financial ease, but also opened up many exciting vistas of art, theatre and music in Delhi. From a total recluse moving among monuments of the past, I was suddenly in a new world of art and culture, along with many new friends.

On a stage equipped with superb lighting equipment and props, plays such as Tagore's *Rakta Karabi* or *Heer Ranjha* by Sheila Bhatia were experiences that could not be easily forgotten. Even among English plays, *Tea House of the August Moon*, or Pirandello's *Six Characters in Search of an Author,* left a profound impression, with their lighting effects by my new friend Sitangshu Mukherji. It was also good fun to climb up to the lighting control panel and see Sitangshu handling rows of lighting dimmers like a pianist.

On the same stage I had an interesting experience of photographing more than one performance of Indrani Rehman, a pioneer Odissi dancer of great calibre. One or two of those photographs, which were my early experiments with colour, made it to the cover and pages of a popular illustrated magazine of that age called *The Illustrated Weekly of India*, published by *The Times of India* group from Mumbai. Connected with Indrani's dance photographs I had an unusual meeting with

■ Pandit Nehru with Barada Ukil, Chairman, AIFACS, 1957

the legendary figure of modern Indian art, MF Husain, and what a comedy of errors it turned out to be!

A week or two after Indrani Rehman's dance recital, her husband Habib-ur-Rehman, a gifted architect, rang me up and asked to see those pictures soon. He rather kindly invited me for tea to their flat at Sujan Singh Park. So, on the appointed afternoon as I rang the door bell punctually, a tall person with a salt-and-pepper beard and bare feet opened the door. His crumpled grey trousers and rather wild look made me think very imprudently that he was the cook of the family and I asked him if his sahib and memsahib were at home.

However, Habib rushed out at that precise moment, and introduced me to the greatest of Indian painters, Maqbul Fida Husain. I still blush in shame when I happen to recall that enigmatic smile on his face, on that particular afternoon. A few years later I saw him often, roaming about in a T-model Ford car, painted in psychedelic colours. I think he was making his innovative documentary film, *Through the Eyes of a Painter* that year.

The International Exhibition of Contemporary Art began with a good deal of fanfare in February 1957 and many of my photographs were in constant demand both by embassies and by the foreign press. Though Pandit Nehru could not be present at the opening ceremony, he dropped in quite casually one day. Barada Ukil, the chairman of AIFACS, sent me an SOS to cover this visit. That was my first opportunity to photograph the Prime Minister of India. He came to the exhibition in a large black car, probably a Cadillac, or a Lincoln, and was accompanied by a single police escort riding a motorbike.

It was once again at the same exhibition and also in the AIFACS hall, that I met many great artists of different schools such as Professor Bhabesh Sanyal, Satish Gujral and the gifted sculptor Dhanraj Bhagat. The well-known art critic of Delhi, Charles Fabri, introduced me to Dhanraj Bhagat and asked us to work together for a book on sculptures. Though I took some interesting pictures of some of his sculptures, the book somehow failed to take off and all I have are some photographic records of this sculptor's works.

Shortly afterwards, I got an opportunity to photograph the new campus of Kirori Mal College designed by Professor CHS Jhabwala, who came to visit my father often with his wife, the novelist Ruth Prawar Jhabwala. As a matter of fact that was the time when my illustrious father had become known after his first visit to England. We had a stream of literary celebrities and diplomats visiting our flat at Mori Gate. At times it was rather odd to see more than one luxury car – the French Ambassador's Jaguar, the Canadian High Commissioner's Cadillac, a Rolls Royce from the British High Commission – parked before our house.

Among the noted literary figures, I remember Nobel Prize winners such as Sir VS Naipaul, the Mexican poet Dr Antonio Paz and the Italian novelist Alberto Moravia. Also a literary critic, Professor IA Richard and poet Stephen Spender along with family friends such as Khushwant Singh could often be seen at our flat.

While working at AIFACS, I discovered the influence which certain officials, and some of the embassies, had on many artists and

Mrs Khushwant Singh with daughter Mala, 1958

intellectuals who came flocking to Delhi. The so-called cultural acadamies, along with leading art societies, were supposed to be governed by elected members, but the crucial financial controls were always vested in officials from the old ICS or IAS cadre, and they had rather strong inclinations of their own. These officials went on dispensing favours according to their likes and even stronger dislikes. But on the whole nearly all cultural centres and art societies did flourish in spite of these pitfalls and had diverse programmes to their credit.

Some of the embassies and high commissions functioning from New Delhi had their own agenda for granting fellowships and travel grants. These were usually dispensed according to the different political blocks to which artists or authors belonged. Quite a few of such cultural sponsors were camouflaged so well with lofty names that, let alone minnows like me, even big names could not infer that those cultural organisations had political overtones.

It was somewhat distressing to attend some of the cultural evenings organised by embassies and foreign information centres. While one could see a film classic such as *Battleship Potemkin*, many leading names from the cultural and intellectual circles of Delhi often were more interested in the various delicacies served during the cultural events of those days.

Then one Sunday afternoon when I answered the doorbell, I was completely overwhelmed to see the impressive figure of Satyajit Ray, the film-maker. He had just won his first international laurel at Cannes Film Festival for *Pather Panchali*. He was a personality rather well-known to us from our Kolkata days. He dropped in often those days to hear my father's records of western classical music and years later in his autobiography had a very nice comment on me. It so happened that I could spot one of the famous quartets of Hayden at the young age of seven.

He was also kind enough to look through some of my photographs and advised me to introduce some local people and colour in my photographs of old architecture and historic cities. That advice made me quite determined to go ahead with my plans to visit the forgotten city with the golden fort, Jaisalmer. But, as there were still a few days more to work at AIFACS, I thought of dropping in at the Old Secretariat to see why my feature on Indian Railways was not appearing in *Yojana*.

What I came to know from a fellow photojournalist was that my photographs were considered rather too pictorial and they lacked the required emphasis on India's Five-Year Plans. It was a policy-level decision about which I certainly had no competence to judge. But it did dampen my spirit. No one at that government organisation seemed to be interested in my project on the golden citadel of Jaisalmer, hidden among the sand dunes of the Thar desert.

However, while chatting with fellow photographers at the Publications Division, I picked up the news that the School of Town and Country Planning, which later became the well-known School of Planning and Architecture, had a vacancy for a photographer with some experience of photographing architecture and old and new towns. After looking up the exact job requirement in a newspaper, I typed out an application. I attached some clippings of my published features and left the packet at the school's first office functioning from Mansingh Road.

After that there was very little work for me in Delhi and straightaway I began my first trip as a back-packer to Jodhpur and Jaisalmer. As for financing that trip, including buying colour films, I collected a prize of hundred rupees from the Railway Board for a pictorial rendering of a steam locomotive, which I had taken in my misplaced enthusiasm for *Yojana*. And though it has always been Delhi that has been the centre of my world, I was excited about my new venture. I left for Rajasthan with a bag full of hope and optimism.

Chapter 14

In a Flash

Author on Ring Road, 1962

In a Flash

Soon, I bought a tiny Lambretta scooter to roam all over Delhi with my cameras and my wife-to-be. She, at that time, was picking up the essential rudiments of photography with zeal

On my return from an incredible trip to Jodhpur and Jaisalmer, I found a letter from the School of Town and Country Planning. It asked me to appear for a practical test on photography at the Old Secretariat building and then for an interview at the school's office at the Mansingh Road hutments. The letter was surprisingly polite for a government document and was signed by the director himself. That was rather unusual even in those relaxed days of the late fifties. This letter somehow made me feel optimistic about my future. As I went about diligently to put together an album of my best photographs of Delhi, a sudden problem arose from a least expected source.

A close friend of my father's, who happened to be working as a senior artist at the Publications Division, came to visit us one evening. He casually mentioned to my father that another aspiring photographer had been more or less selected for the job at the School of Town Planning. My interview and tests were merely a formality. This was enough to make my father fly into a rage and he warned me not to go anywhere near the Old Secretariat. That injunction was followed by an implied threat of throwing me out of 'his' house if not obeyed.

Distressed, I took shelter in the calm sanctuary of the Cambridge Brotherhood at Court Lane in Civil Lines. Once there, Reverend James Stuart of that Mission was exceedingly kind. His suggestion was to face the situation in a calm frame of mind. He also promised to talk to my father about allowing me to take my own decisions regarding my prospective jobs.

A few days later, when I was gathering up my camera equipment and getting ready, my father happened to walk into my room and rather casually told me to go ahead with my interviews and test. At last, after many days of tension and anxiety, I could eat my breakfast. Though that May morning was hot, I reached the photo unit of the Publications Division in a cool and determined frame of mind.

After a short session of introductions and briefings, a young Sikh photographer, who was more interested in the latest photo equipment rather than in taking photographs, let all the candidates go around the good old Secretariat building with cameras to search for pictures to show their skills. While my fellow aspirants for that job began to search for interesting angles of that old colonial building, I managed to capture many of the characteristic features of that place without much trouble. Apart from photographing the sprawling building as it stood, I tried to introduce some human angles to my pictorial essay.

In those hot and dry summer days of Delhi, a platoon of men, especially hired, kept fragrant grass screens called khas khas wet by throwing water on them. Those were the days when only a few top officials could have coolers in their rooms, and no air-conditioners could be seen. For me this human angle in my photo story proved to be a scoop, and made me score well in my test.

Next day at the interview I was told that my picture story was good, and the Director, Professor TJ Manickam, a well-known architect and town planner himself, questioned me about my 'Stones of Delhi' article and the one on Lutyens' New Delhi. After a few days I went to the Publications Division to collect my negatives and got the good news from Mr Kasinath himself that I had made the grade and should expect the job offer soon. After joining the School of Town and Country Planning, I could observe the area around India Gate quite closely. The bus stop where I usually got down was right next to King George's statue which, at that time, was very much in position under the tall canopy. One evening I was rather surprised to notice that scaffoldings had come up under that canopy, and many workmen were swarming all over the marble statue of the British king. Luckily, I carried a camera that day, and lost no time in capturing that non-repeatable scene.

Initially my main work at the School of Planning was to prepare slides from illustrations printed in books. But with the coming of cool weather and a change in the teaching programme, I got a chance to go out. I visited some of villages around Mehrauli. Among those Delhi villages, Chhattarpur and Khanpur on the Mehrauli-

Indraprastha Estate, 1958

Badarpur road, were the ones which I chose for detailed study.

Now, at least a dozen bus routes touch Chhattarpur located almost next to the four-lane highway to Gurgaon. But, at the beginning of 1958, to reach that village one had to walk all the way from the bus terminal inside the Mehrauli hamlet, and go past an interesting old monument called Jahaz Mahal built next to the lake, Hauz Shamsi. There were many old ruins around that lake, and once that picturesque spot had many summer houses and palaces of Mughal kings including Emperor Bahadur Shah Zafar and noblemen. After coming out of Mehrauli, everyone had to trudge through a

■ Zamrudpur, 1963

dusty track to reach Chhattarpur and another village called Sultanpur. There were no signs to indicate the way to these villages; while every old monument, well-known or not, had a stone signpost in its vicinity.

Once one entered either of these twin villages they had the typical appearance of a North Indian village with clusters of mud or brick houses built according to the financial status of their owners. There was also more than one village well, and an open, and colonnaded community hall called chaupal, along with muddy ponds, mainly for buffalos to wallow in. If I remember correctly, the students from the school had to pay special attention to a small but popular temple, which today has turned into a lively pilgrimage spot near Delhi, attracting devotees on certain auspicious days.

While returning from those two villages, I often took the longer route to the Qutb Minar entrance instead of the bus terminus at Mehrauli. On that narrow road first came a fifteenth century mosque called Jamali Kamali with the builder Jamali Khan's tomb just next to that lonely mosque. The tomb had a fantastic ceiling with painted plasterwork, which had survived the depredation of time and can still be seen intact. All round Jamali Masjid there were remains of ruined houses and from the construction pattern they appeared to be residential. In one of them there was an ascetic who treated some of the common ailments such as arthritis with water filled in different coloured bottles. Once he told me proudly that the result of his treatment could be judged by making his patients climb the towering Qutb Minar.

Some of those ruins patched up in the fifties became the first office and shelters of the Youth Hostel movement where I did some voluntary work as an early member in 1954. On the other side of the road, on a hillock, was a dark Tughlaq tomb with a dome, and a tiny stone castle popularly known as Metcalfe's Battery, which had nothing to do with the artillery or guns.

In contrast, the subject of my assignment to the village Khanpur in April 1958 was rather unusual and had a touch of comedy. I was asked to photograph the impact of an electric generator powered by a pair of bullocks, as that village was still without a supply of electricity. That innovative project was the brainchild of an expert sponsored by an American aid agency. When I reached that village after travelling in a private bus, I found an American guzzling canned beer from a bright red icebox along with his assistant. At a nearby barren field a pair of bullocks, while tethered to an electric generator set, were driven hard by two local villagers dressed in dhotis and turbans.

Such frantic efforts by both animals and men showed up as a faint glow of electric lights fixed to a pole, and also as a thin trickle of water flowing out of an electric pump fixed to a village well. Though I tried to create a picture of that rural experiment, which looked tangible, yet that pioneering project near Delhi for rural electrification appeared to be a non-starter.

In the summer of 1959, the School of Town and Country Planning moved to its new premises at Indraprastha Estate, right next to the Ring Road. Before us only a few other government buildings had been built and the vast Income Tax Office, or ITO for short, was the first office to start functioning in that area where wild scrublands with many patches of wet swamps abounded with a variety of wildlife. There is a reference in the Bhagavat Purana about the Indraprastha of ancient times, and some of those descriptions closely matched that area along the Yamuna.

In our young days, though we took liberties with many other wild areas around Delhi,

■ Purana Qila, 1961
(taken by Malabika Chaudhuri)

those wet patches south of Rajghat, and behind Purana Qila, were left strictly alone for fear of snakes, crocodiles, and even wild pigs. Sometimes we would see from the Qila-i-Kuhna mosque of the Old Fort, a few herds of sturdy nilgai or blue bulls grazing on that wet land.

The last Mughal Emperor, Bahadur Shah Zafar, did most of his shikar trips across the Yamuna, rather than Indraprastha Estate, and that was probably because the area was quite tough for him at the age of seventy-seven.

From my office window high up on the Town Planning building, I could see a vast landscape towards the old gates of Purana Qila and the majestic white dome of Humayun's Tomb. Only the Ring Road, which had been completed a few years before, wound its way right up to the villages of Kilokri and Ashram next to Mathura Road.

Towards the north, the ruins of Feroz Shah Kotla with the Ashoka Pillar on top provided another historic view from my new office at IP Estate.

At Pandit Nehru's funeral, 1964

A couple of years later, the department of architecture was integrated with the town planning school, and the premier institute functioning in Delhi was renamed the School of Planning and Architecture or SPA. The merging of these two teaching institutions of similar disciplines had an important beneficial effect on me. I was promoted as an instructor and became part of the teaching faculty of the school. Soon, I bought a tiny Lambretta scooter to roam all over Delhi with my cameras and my wife-to-be. At that time, she was picking up the essential rudiments of photography with zeal.

We began to frequent the vast open area of Delhi Zoo and while I kept the single-lens reflex camera with a telephoto lens to myself, my pupil had to be satisfied with an old Rolleicord camera, which she managed to use rather well. One of her pictures showed a group of elephants against a Purana Qila gate. This unusual shot was soon published in the pages of an English daily as a lead picture of a weekly feature called 'New Delhi Notebook'. Delhi Zoo was a good experiment as an open-enclosured zoo, and its entire landscaping was done by a young Japanese architect called Hatashita.

I got married in 1962 and moved to a small place near Nizam-ud-Din and later to a South Delhi colony called Amar Colony, beyond the main Ring Road. Amar Colony was an area meant for people who after Partition had camped for years inside Purana Qila. They were finally allotted land near Lady Shri Ram College for Women in South Delhi. Our house belonged to a Sindhi doctor who had moved out of Delhi for his practice. The location of that first-floor flat was at the end of that modest, yet decent colony. There was a large rocky area across our house which has now become the prosperous East of Kailash neighbourhood.

There were two villages, Zamrudpur and Garhi, on two sides of our colony, and we would often see village women trudging to a village located in front of Lady Shri Ram College. Little did I know then that my daughter would complete her university education from that college itself and we would live at a nearby house in Kailash Colony for more than thirty years. More than forty years ago, many jackals would howl all night from the direction of a hillock where, at present, the ISKCON temple is located. Yet the whole area in the early sixties was so safe that we did not hear of a single burglary or violent incident, which seemed to have become a norm these days.

One May afternoon of 1964, while eating lunch with my colleagues at the office canteen, we heard the sad news that Pandit Jawaharlal Nehru had died of a stroke that morning. Every workplace, government or private, was declared closed. When going home, an old villager stopped me and asked if the news that "Nehru Maharaj" had expired was true. On getting an affirmation from me, he struck his forehead with his hand and exclaimed, "What will happen to our country, Bharat! Bad days were certainly ahead!"

The state funeral for the first Prime Minister of India was scheduled for the next day. We heard that Dharam Vira, the chief of Delhi's Administration, was preparing a swampy piece of land north of Rajghat for the state funeral. Though tempted at first, I had no inclination to photograph that tragic event. But, around noon, a picture agency from Paris contacted me through the French Embassy and asked me to cover the ceremony for an important magazine.

■ The last rites at Pandit Nehru's funeral, 1964

I had to rush out of our flat with a camera and some colour films, which I had been saving for my next trip to the hills. The only credentials that I had for covering that epoch-making story was a copy of the cable from the news agency, duly forwarded by the French Embassy.

In those days of relaxed security I could go right up to the funeral enclosure which was jammed with dignitaries such as President Dr Radhakrishnan, acting PM Gulzari Lal Nanda and the next PM Lal Bahadur Shastri. The young grandson of the late Pandit Nehru, Rajiv Gandhi, was there and he completed all the funeral rites. Jostling in that VIP crowd were Lord and Lady Mountbatten with the British Prime Minister in a long morning coat and a top hat. Among many Asian statesmen I remember seeing President Sukarno from Indonesia. It was one of the hottest days in Delhi, with the mercury well above the forties. It must have indeed been a gruelling test for all those leading political figures from all over the world, dressed in heavy formal clothes. On my part, it took a good deal of effort and some borrowed money to complete that assignment.

A year later I got another assignment from a leading newspaper in London where I was asked to photograph the various aspects of post-Independent Delhi. This made me go all over Delhi starting from those refugee tenements called Old Double Storeys, where occupants kept cattle for fresh milk on the ground floor and usually hung out their string beds during the day from their first-floor balconies. At the other end of the spectrum, I photographed some of the smart houses of Golf Links and Defence Colony.

Once, while driving my scooter over a new flyover above the railway line near Jangpura, I came across an elephant striding along that modern flyover. It was a subject that could just not be missed and, as I took out my camera, an Ambassador car drove up the flyover. In that moment I could capture a rare combination of transport, old and new. The resulting picture was immediately selected as the lead picture on Indian scenes after Independence and on New Delhi.

My other favourite subjects at that time were the new embassy buildings at Chanakyapuri. It is amazing to think now how I could just walk right inside those embassies, including the new American Embassy designed by Edward Stone. I could even set up my camera on a tripod inside at night, and give long exposures for flood-lit buildings, without any fuss. Only at the Pakistan High Commission, the security people were always around and took care to note down my scooter number.

I never realised that India's first war with Pakistan would break out so soon. The entire atmosphere in Delhi, and all over India, changed in a flash. One evening my wife and I were enjoying a hard-earned dinner at a new Chinese restaurant, which had become rather fashionable, and all of a sudden the lights went off. At first we took it as a power failure, but soon learnt that a blackout was clamped on the capital as Ambala City was under air attack. We paid our bills in candlelight and drove home slowly with only the tail lights on.

When we were about to reach our house my little scooter ran into a pile of sand left on the road by a building contractor. Both of us fell down in a heap, and though not seriously hurt, the incident did create some scare, and we even thought of disposing of my two-wheeled vehicle.

I now began to concentrate on photographing the Himalayan hills. As for my official work, it comprised either teaching practical photography to a group not interested in the subject, or it was a routine job of photographing government housing projects, which I found to be rather unexciting.

Finally, early in 1968 when our daughter was only a few months old, my wife and I decided to leave Amar Colony. After trying to settle all over Delhi, from Mori Gate to the Medical Institute, we finally moved into a small, but smart, flat in the tranquil Kailash Colony in South Delhi.

Chapter 15

The Return

Jangpura flyover, 1965

The Return

More than three decades after I ceased to work seriously on Delhi, this capital city with its myriad of facets and activities once again came to my rescue. On January 24, 2001, I had an occasion to go up the majestic steps of Rashtrapati Bhawan on Raisina Hill

It was an early March morning of 1998 and I was about to land at the Indira Gandhi Airport of Delhi. The twin-engine jet plane, which is far more comfortable for economy-class passengers than a sardine-packed Jumbo Jet, had left Copenhagen late in the evening. Even at that early hour I could see the whole of South Delhi as the plane followed its landing path. The landscape below was more or less a solid mass of bricks and concrete with all too few oases of green parks, or monuments surrounded by lawns. Right at some distance I could vaguely discern the three pink spires of a temple and a neighbourhood park, only a short distance from my little flat at Kailash Colony.

One of the reasons that I had to cut short my stay at Oxford, and was also prevented from attending on my century-old father, was this flat in South Delhi. I had been living there for close to thirty years and had to face no end of trouble from the usual Delhi phenomenon of tenant versus owner relationships. The entire South Delhi, along with our colony, had turned into a concrete jungle of multi-storeyed flats. The view from the window of my aeroplane closely resembled an early photograph of Shajahanabad taken in 1858 by Felice Beato from one of the high minars above the Jama Masjid.

The resemblance was far too close for comfort. The only thing, which neither my aerial view nor the old photograph, could express was the acute shortage of a healthy water supply and the overflowing of sewage systems in two areas of Delhi, separated by a gap of a century-and-a- half. My wife and daughter, staying in New Delhi, had not only to fight a daily battle for the supply of a few buckets of clean water, but were also facing the threat of frequent electricity breakdowns. In addition, many neighbours who had more than one car would often barge into our driveway, even at the middle of the night, and park their vehicles with no hint of apology or scruple.

With the sudden sound of the wheels of my plane being lowered and the screaming of jet engines at landing pitch, I could catch a glimpse of the new campus of the Indian Institute of Mass Communication at the fringe of Jawaharlal Nehru University. I had a long association with that Institute and even after retiring as a regular faculty member in 1993, I continued to teach there as visiting faculty till the summer of 1997.

As chance would have it, I had changed my job in early 1969, soon after moving into our new residence at Kailash Colony. It was rather tough at first to cope with the triple challenge of a new residence, a strange place of work, as well as attending to the needs of a baby daughter born a good five years after our marriage. However, my wife and I did manage to cope with most of our difficulties with a good deal of optimism. Since my parents had gone away to England at that time, many of the crucial decisions regarding our life and my new job in Delhi had to be taken entirely on our own. But the wonderful atmosphere around our two-roomed flat and the presence of many friendly neighbours, young and old, went a long way in making our life in South Delhi pleasant.

Kailash Colony was one of the earliest efforts of an enterprising private coloniser of New Delhi. During my college days I had often seen a black Hudson car ferrying prospective buyers from Connaught Place to the barren rocky landscape of Kailash Colony and to the swampy area of Model Town near the Coronation Park in North Delhi. One of the main attractions of Kailash Colony was the setting up of a public school by Reverend JJ Tytler, a prominent educationist of Delhi. A landmark of our colony was a low hillock with a temple, which I tried to spot every time when flying into Delhi.

Though we had moved into that colony more than a decade after it had come up, it was still far from being crowded and was inhabited by families with modest, yet decent means. There were three green parks within walking distance from our house. One of those parks had a shallow pond and an enormous banyan tree, over a century old. That pond as well as the old ficus retusa tree had been a part of the nearby village of Zamrudpur. In the month of

July, village women dressed in bright clothes fixed their swings from the branches of this banyan tree and swayed gaily to the rhythm of folk songs of the festival of Teej.

There was also a neighbourhood shopping centre around one of the parks. Every evening we would combine our daily shopping with a leisurely ramble. Since Kailash Colony had many Bengali house-owners, a fishmonger from Gujarat did a roaring business here. But at the turn of this century this shop disappeared. For noodles or fried rice we walked over to a solitary Chinese restaurant of South Delhi. After returning home on summer nights, we could safely sleep in our little garden-cum-driveway without the least fear. It may sound incredible but once, in 1972, all of us went to Corbett Park and Ranikhet, forgetting to lock our door. On our return, we found that not a single object was missing.

But many decades later, in March or April 1998, there were two cases of shoot-outs and stabbing right inside our block. I was seriously ill at that time, with symptoms of acute food-poisoning. However, Dr Tarun Chatterjee, who had treated me earlier, in 1991, put me on the drip without delay. As I lay in half-stupor in a nursing home in Kailash Colony, my mind was working like a video-editing machine running in reverse about my twenty-four-year stint at the Indian Institute of Mass Communication.

From the second-floor window of my office I could see right across to Kotla Mubarakpur and the interesting dome of Mubarak Shah's tomb. The traffic on Ring Road was not only thin, but at times one had to wait for a good part of an hour before one could get a bus to Kailash Colony. Once again, I took to walking home on winter evenings, passing the old Moth-ki-Masjid and the cauliflower fields behind the government quarters of Andrewsgunj and the houses of Greater Kailash.

After spending eighteen years in that building in South Extension, the institute shifted to its own campus at the Jawaharlal Nehru University. The campus was both lonely and arid. In the evenings we could often see a nilgai jumping over the low boundary wall.

Through my tenure here I had many challenging assignments, particularly during the directorship of MV Desai and HY Sharda Prasad. At times I felt the atmosphere rather stifling and sometimes downright hostile. Those unexpected bouts of tension at the workplace, combined with the stress of living in New Delhi, made me want to escape – to as far as Yorkshire in England or to a small town called Samchi in South Bhutan. But every time I nearly succeeded in moving away from both IIMC and New Delhi, something or the other, typical of this capital city and its politics, made it imperative for me to return to Delhi like a haunted character depicted in Rabindra Nath Tagore's story *Hungry Stones*.

In 1971, while training for TV programme-production techniques at the University of York, I received a good offer to work as a trainee television producer with a good stipend and accommodation. But before anything could be finalised, the news of the imminent Bangladesh war made my parents and my historian brother, who were supporting me in England, so jittery that they asked me return to India without any delay.

Twelve years later, once again, I managed to escape to the National Institute of Education of the Royal Government of Bhutan on a UNESCO-sponsored project. In less than a year, Operation Blue Star in the Punjab had a strong repercussion even in the distant border towns of North Bengal and Bhutan, and the Gorkhaland Movement made me finally abandon my idyllic stay at Bhutan. I had no other alternative but to reduce my stay in Bhutan to a single academic year instead of three, and fly back to Delhi for the sake of my daughter's school education as well as my wife's health.

On returning to Delhi in the autumn of 1984, I found the city completely changed. There were flyovers everywhere, completed for the Asian Games, and a rise in road traffic with the first people's car, the Maruti. That three-cylinder car was entering Delhi streets, and everyone worthy of the name had either wanted to have a car of their own, or sold their booking rights at a high premium.

The other change that greeted my eyes, particularly all over South Delhi, was the many multi-storeyed flats built by pulling down individual bungalows and double-storeyed houses. This created a mad rush to push poor tenants out by all possible means.

Another change was in the television programmes and the opening of more than a single channel for Delhi. This rapid expansion had begun mainly with the coming in of soap operas such as *Hum Log*, *Buniyaad* and religious serials such as the *Ramayana* and the *Mahabharata*. Though the advent of satellite and cable television was yet almost a decade ahead, no media pandits were prepared to listen to my plea made in 1985 that television programmes, both news as well as entertainment, beamed down from a satellite, were likely to have a profound influence on our media, as well as on society.

To sum up the media scene, and also what was happening to Delhi at the turn of the new century, let me quote from a piece of writing which I did towards the end of 2001, but somehow never got down to publishing it:

"On the third day of the new millennium I was invited to join the New Year's celebration by my dynamic young colleague, Professor Jayashri Jethwani, at the campus of the Mass Communication Institute where I used to teach. After being greeted warmly by many members of the faculty and staff I went up to the top of the new teaching block to see the view.

"Once the entire landscape around the JNU campus was barren and rocky. Yet at the beginning of the new century trees planted over the last ten years had flourished to give a wonderful dense green look. But what had particularly interested me from that high spot was a large number of satellite dishes and wireless masts visible over many buildings, including the Delhi IIT, as well important buildings of the JNU, including the Mass Communication Institute...

"After photographing some of those communication devices, which have become essential to our life all over this capital city, I suddenly observed a group of men and women construction workers relaxing before their thatched shanties right within the campus of the institute. The weak winter sun gave a wonderful glowing look to their humble abode and daily activities. Standing there on a balcony of the Mass Communication Institute, I could not resist but take a quick shot with my camera to capture that scene, which has become very common at many of the construction sites seen in New Delhi.

"The contrast between the simple and stark living conditions of those people surrounded by all technological developments seemed to be a dichotomy, which was present all over Delhi, and yet difficult to explain even at the beginning of this century...

"More than three decades, after I ceased to work seriously on Delhi, this capital city with its myriad facets and activities once again came to my rescue. On January 24, 2001, I had occasion to go up the majestic steps of Rashtrapati Bhawan on Raisina Hill. An invitation to attend a ceremony at Ashoka Hall had arrived and in that imposing hall a new illustrated book on New Delhi was about to be presented to the President.

"Before entering the portals of that majestic building one of the officials, after scrutinising my invitation card as well as a proof of identity, asked for my mobile phone as a matter of duty. When I told him that I had none, he gave me a puzzled look in disbelief, and waived me on to a security guard.

"While the guard was busy doing his duty with a metal detector, I could not help but look at a nearby counter, where more than a dozen cell phones lay neatly tagged but staring rather uselessly at the towering columns designed by Lutyens.

"Though the invitation card had mentioned quite clearly that no mobile phones would be allowed inside the ceremonial hall, most of the VIP guests could never think of parting with their inseparable electronic companions even for an hour or two. This was typical of many politicians, high officials and media personalities of 21st century Delhi. Once seated inside Ashoka Hall, which was the main ballroom of British Viceroys, I could see on the balcony above a row of trumpeters from the Guards, who were standing alert to herald the Head of the State with a fanfare of their brass instruments.

"The scene in the glittering hall of Rashtrapati Bhawan was very similar to the scene at Diwan-i-Khas in the evenings at the time of Shah Jahan's rule, and as described by historian Banarsi Prasad Saksena in his wonderful book on the life of Shah Jahan.

"But, along with this spectacular show of tradition, in a corner of the same hall, a battery of television cameramen were ready with their latest betacam and digital equipment to show the ceremony immediately on numerous television channels beaming down from more than one satellite. The contrast of the old and the new seen at the Presidential House that evening was once again a characteristic feature seen everywhere at the very beginning of the 21st century Delhi."

That piece of writing was done at our Mayur Vihar flat where, thanks to the generosity of my daughter Satarupa, we could move in towards the end of 1998. And with that move all my dreams of settling elsewhere other than my native Delhi simply vanished. Though we moved to a third floor of a cooperative housing complex and to the other bank of the Yamuna, the fresh air blowing through our flat all day and peacocks calling every morning, went a long way to support our decision for moving to the area of Delhi called Yamuna Paar. This name given to all developments on the eastern bank of the river was attributed mainly by all true-blooded citizens of Delhi. But, with the running of the latest Metro rail service from Shahdara of the eastern bank, the Yamuna Paar, along with the new Noida City in Uttar Pradesh can no longer be treated lightly.

Epilogue
A Wide Angle

Kashmere Gate, 1955

A Wide Angle

Sitting in the dark verandah which, like the teddy bear Winnie the Pooh, happens to be my thoughtful spot, I realised, almost like Mirza Ghalib, that Delhi, both the old and the new, had given me all that I cherish today

On February 21, 2003, I was woken up early in the morning by a pair of Indian robins whistling for their daily quota of biscuit crumbs from my chhota hazri. Immediately, a voice muffled by many layers of blankets and quilts piped, "Happy Birthday" from a bed habitually occupied by my wife, Malabika. So there I was, in no way could I forget that having reached the proverbial biblical age of three score and ten, every single day afterwards was likely to be counted as a bonus.

Stepping on to the front verandah for giving a birthday treat to my feathered friends, I saw the sun shining brightly across the river Yamuna near Mayur Vihar in East Delhi. There was an immediate impulse to go out with a camera and visit Old Delhi and also the Ridge before joining the family for a birthday lunch at Connaught Place. By the time I managed to come out of our housing complex and reach the bus stop on Noida Road, it was already a few minutes past nine. Soon, I was scooped up into a crowded chartered bus by the conductor, who went on shouting expletives at another van, popularly known as an RTV. While crossing the Nizamuddin Bridge, our bus had to cope with a heavy traffic snarl crawling over the crowded bridge, and with other unexpected stops created by the security barriers put up by the city police. During one of those forced stops, the stench that was emanating from the stagnant river and from an open garbage truck on MCD duty became rather unpleasant, to say the least.

To escape that strong assault on my nostrils, I tried to look out of the bus window, and what I saw was a typical traffic jam seen often in this capital city. The pedestrian causeway on the left was packed with many rows of scooters and motorbikes astride with drivers wearing crash helmets of all colours. Those headgears made the drivers look like an army of aliens invading Delhi, the old and the new. This somewhat bizarre but common sight seen often in Delhi was made even more bizarre by a number of women sitting on the pillion, dressed in bright saris and salwar suits. Today a Rip Van Winkle crossing the river at this very spot near Patpargunj village, where two hundred years ago Delhi was lost to the British, would never have believed that the scene on the river bank was real and not a dream.

It was a few minutes past ten when I could at last manage to tumble out of that crowded bus near the Cottage Industries Emporium on Janpath. I had to rush into a nearby American fast-food joint, more for their shiny and clean toilets rather than a cup of coffee. But as there was no intention on my part of taking undue advantage of that excellent facility, not easily found in Connaught Place, I sat down with a paper cup of mocha coffee and looked out of a glass window onto Janpath. It came to my mind that the same place was once the showroom of ES Pearey Lal, the motorwala. Apart from selling cars right from the early part of the last century, this gentleman happened to be a prominent public figure of British Delhi. Till the late forties, that particular showroom on Janpath had many American cars such as an Oldsmobile, a Buick, and even a Chevrolet, for sale.

After finishing my coffee, I walked down the good old Queen's Way and soon stopped at a shop where the India Coffee House was once located. It was famous for serving refreshments to many cash-starved intellectuals and budding artists like me. While the coffee house had been turned into a glittering jeweller's shop, beckoning the rich, a signboard on the first floor announced that the first art school of Delhi was still functioning under the name of a well-known Bengali artist Saroda Ukil. Further down Queen's Way, and at the corner of Scindia House, was another showroom for cars which specialised in dealing with elegant Rolls Royces and Bentleys during the British Imperial days.

At that time, three or four of those aristocratic cars could always be seen parked inside that showroom.Around them a few English salesmen strutted about like male peacocks, dressed in impeccable three-piece suits. There was this story of the Maharaja of Alwar, famous for his whimsical ways, who got furious when treated in an offhand manner by one of those British salesmen. To take revenge, the Maharaja bought every Rolls Royce in that showroom and used them for towing garbage, including night soil, in his princely state of Alwar in Rajasthan. Standing before the same showroom, I could not help but smile at a signboard above the entrance, where the once two big Rs of Rolls Royce ruled. Now, from the same place, a signboard announced that the showroom was selling the people's car, Maruti.

Then, at the corner of the underground market called Palika Bazaar, I decided to board a station wagon service still called phut-phatis. This shared system of transport from Connaught Place to Red Fort was once run by hefty Harley Davidson motorbikes, towing passenger vehicles built like the tongas of Old Delhi. They got their weird name from the loud spluttering sound emitted by their open twin-cylinder engines. More often than not, these vehicles used to be driven by burly Sikh drivers who flocked to Delhi in 1947.

The phut-phati van that I had got into raced down Minto Bridge and drove along Asaf Ali Road, which was built after smashing the old wall of Shahjahanabad. The Turkman Gate named after an ancient saint stood intact, but could hardly be recognised because of the congestion and chaotic traffic. After turning into Daryagunj at Delhi Gate, we stopped near a lane next to a cinema house called Golcha. There I tried to catch a quick glimpse of the old Naharwali Haveli, which had shot into media fame as the childhood house of General Musharraf, the President of Pakistan.

After reaching the bird hospital at the famous Lal Mandir situated at the beginning of Chandni Chowk, I got down from the van and went to take a look at the famous Palace of Begum Samru, the Indian wife of the German mercenary, Walter Reinhart. This particular building, now known as Bhagirath Palace, could once be seen easily from the main road. The entire building is surrounded by many ugly shacks. But the name of a British bank, Lloyds Bank, painted on the pediment at the top, can still be seen, along with the old Venetian blinds crumbling with age.

At this point of my excursion into the old city, I tried to engage an auto driver who would be ready to take me to Pir Ghaib on the Ridge. But the general behaviour of these drivers in Delhi is more strange than that of the March Hare in the tale of Alice in Wonderland. Finally, I decided to go aboard a cycle rickshaw. On boarding that human-powered vehicle, I discovered that it was one of the best mobile platforms for my photography and for exploring an over-crowded city such as Shahjahanabad.

With a few powerful strokes on the twin pedals, my rickshaw driver propelled his vehicle through that road crowded with transport of all kinds. He stopped just before the railway bridge, once known as the Lothian Bridge. Right across the road I could see the little Catholic church of St. Mary's inside a convent school. At that particular crossing, waiting for the traffic light to turn green, stood an elephant bearing some advertising banners.

On my left, riding a cycle rickshaw, was an unusually tall woman dressed in a shiny blue sari. A quick and surreptitious glance in that direction was enough to realise that the person was a kinnaur or hermaphrodite. After having read Khushwant Singh's novel *Delhi*, I could not help but marvel at these traditional symbolic figures who are still flourishing in Delhi. Suddenly, there was a faint electronic beep from the rickshaw on my left, and as the elephant began to flap its ears at the noise, the hermaphrodite took out a mobile phone from the folds of the sari and shouted in a rather gruff voice, "Haan, kya hai?"or "Yes, what is it?"

With the traffic light turning green, all of us, including the elephant, moved on. The view after the dark arches of the Lothian Bridge was an exact depiction of history recorded by Professor Percival Spear and Dr Narayani Gupta. As my cycle rickshaw went up the gentle slope of Lothian Road, the derelict gateway of an old ammunition magazine came into view. Once this was a monument painted spotlessly white in memory of three British officers who blew it up in 1857. Now, with heavy soot deposited by countless railway engines of the loco yard, that gate looked really grim.

On the other side of the road was the first post and telegraph building of Delhi. It looked deceptively new, with a fresh coat of whitewash and green paint. Only the rarely-seen Venetian blinds – no longer in use in modern buildings – gave away the true age of the post office, often visited in my boyhood days.

In those days, I had to visit that post office almost every day, for posting and collecting my father's urgent letters. And, shortly after the troublesome days of 1947, I had to act as an honorary postman for several weeks.

My next stop was near a colonial building inside the campus of the Delhi College of Engineering. This was once the palace and library of Prince Dara Shikoh. After the occupation of Delhi in 1803, it became the first British Residency. Since there was no photograph of this historical building in my collection, I tried very hard to get a good view of it. But my efforts were in vain. Disappointed, I moved on to the partially-demolished hostel called Allnut, and the still intact bungalow, Maitland House, which was built like a castle. Maitland House was once the residence of many teachers of St. Stephen's, including CF Andrews, who was an ardent follower of Mahatma Gandhi and Rabindra Nath Tagore.

From there I turned into Madrasa Road at the corner of St. James' Church. After seeing the churchyard, where James Skinner and William Fraser lay buried, I stopped my rickshaw at the gate of an old bungalow with a curious white dome. This building has become a railway engineering office and the entry there is far from easy. Yet, fifty years ago when the same place was an institute of the Indian Railways, and World War II was still raging, we brothers walked into this old bungalow often to see the Yamuna in flood. Underneath that same bungalow, and on the rampart wall, was a gateway which opened on to Bela Road, next to the river. At times, we would find those rickety doors open and take a hurried look into that dark underground passage leading to a tykhana, or an underground shelter. The fear of snakes and the acrid smell of bat droppings, however, stopped us from going deep into that dungeon which was full of mysteries.

After reading the interesting *City of Djinns* by William Dalrymple, I realised that those underground chambers were the old tykhana, the basement of a palace built by a Mughal nobleman called Ali Mardan Khan. This historic bungalow became the residence of William Fraser, the Deputy Commissioner of Delhi.

My rickshaw driver finally dropped me near an old cinema called Ritz, opposite Kashmere Gate. Gazing around, I could hardly recognise that familiar square. Right before me stood the remnant of the old stone bastion, along with the ultra-modern Metro Station.

From here, I decided to enter the narrow end of Nicholson Road, and travel down memory lane to the P&O Building and Mori Gate. As I walked up the gentle slope before Hassan Building, I found that the area along the old city wall had become very commercial. Our old residence, too, though well-maintained for its age, looked rather forsaken and lonely.

As I was trying to take a shot of our old building with my wide-angle lens, an old man selling tea at a roadside stall called out to me. After an exchange of greetings, he asked whether I used to stay on the top floor, and belonged to Kutta Wallah Sahib's family. Since my father had a huge Alsatian dog, he was always known in our old locality as the "Dog Owner Sahib". On hearing a somewhat surprised affirmative, the old tea stall owner pulled me down on a rickety bench. He would not let me go until I drank a glass of tea made by him. Being one of the last of the refugee families from Pakistan, he had started that tea stall in an alcove of the old city wall long ago.

After finishing the glass of tea, when I tried to pay for it, the man not only refused, but also warned me not to do so again. This surprising experience on my birthday left me almost speechless, and I walked out of Mori Gate marvelling at the humane quality of this fellow citizen of Delhi.

At last, only a short distance into Civil Lines and with a Metro train thundering overhead, I could engage a three-wheeler cab willing enough to take me up to the Northern Ridge. The driver followed Court Road, and I remembered the old bungalow of Cambridge Brotherhood inside Court Lane. Father James Stuart and Reverend Ian Weatherall, vicar of St. James' Church, had been friends of our family and the Mission library had been my refuge during my difficult student days.

After entering Rajpur Road, my driver finally managed to find Hindu Rao Road, winding up the Ridge. The large rock where we watched peacocks and parrots was still there, though fenced by an iron grill. After having a look at the lonely Ashoka pillar, I reached the old ruin of Pir Ghaib.

This monument has now been enclosed within the campus of Hindu Rao Hospital. Many family quarters and a water tank around Pir Ghaib have completely destroyed the old-world charm of this unique monument on the Ridge.

With a heavy heart I got into the auto and set off for the next monument on the Ridge, the Chauburji Masjid. However, the sight of walls and iron fencing everywhere in and around the green forest appeared rather strange and did nothing to improve my mood.

Fortunately, Chauburji Masjid was still peaceful like my college days. The serene atmosphere around the mosque reminded me of wonderful picnic lunches with my college friends Nimai, Nandita, Sarada and Deepali. While coming down the Ridge, my auto driver Pramod could not believe that in that very jungle I had come across a couple of wild animals, probably lakkad baggas or hyenas in plain English. After having come to the end of my trip around Old Delhi, I had to rush towards Connaught Place.

While passing Indraprastha College, I noticed two or three young girls dressed in tight jeans and short tops coming out of the college main gate. The memory of two burqa-clad college girls getting into a special purdah bus of Indraprastha College flashed across my mind. I realised that Delhi, along with its inhabitants, had now moved on to an age which was altogether different.

Approaching Connaught Place, I had to wait for a short while near a state emporium on Baba Khadak Singh Marg, once called Irwin Road. The crowd everywhere was rather cosmopolitan. Motor cars of all makes and measurements were parked like sardines on the pavement. Also visible from that spot were gigantic steel cranes used for constructing the Metro Rail. I missed the shimmering green of many gulmohur trees that flourished there in my young days.

Suddenly there was a long drawn call for the Friday prayer from a loudspeaker fixed atop a nearby mosque. This particular mosque was once an old and neglected ruin. Now people with white caps covering their heads lined up to enter it. A short distance away, and on the opposite side of the road, many red flags were fluttering above one of the oldest temples of Delhi, the Hanuman Mandir. Also, two gurudwaras, along with a church, could be found in that locality of New Delhi.

While returning from my birthday lunch at one of the Chinese restaurants that have mushroomed all over New Delhi, our auto was held up on the Ring Road just before the new Nizamuddin Bridge. The reason for this forced stoppage was due to a long queue of transport vehicles for the newly-introduced fuel, CNG.

Late in the evening, I once again went out to the front verandah, which overlooked the vast landscape across theYamuna. Far away, many lights along the main Ring Road, near the village Kilokri, were just coming on. Those flickering lights reminded me that Kilokri was once the place from where Raja Dilhu ruled in circa 57 BC, and the present name of Delhi is believed to have come from the name of that ancient king.

Sitting in the dark verandah which, like the teddy bear Winnie the Pooh, happens to be my thoughtful spot, I realised, almost like Mirza Ghalib, that Delhi, both the old and the new, had given me all that I cherish today. Had it not been a burning desire to photograph and write about my friends, the tiger and other wild creatures facing extinction, I would have probably, like the Canticle of Simeon in St. Luke's Gospel, exclaimed, "Nunc Dimittis" ("Oh God, let Thy servant depart in peace" and "Amen".)

Acknowledgements

Let me begin by saying to all dear readers, known and unknown, that if you have read and seen my efforts on Delhi, the old and the new, do spare a little more of your patience and time to read this apologia and thanksgiving. When so many authors and historians have written and also illustrated worthy volumes on Delhi, why did I venture on yet another work on this capital city, and that, too, at the good old age of seventy?

This somewhat mad venture began a few years ago with the discovery of a collection of my Delhi negatives and slides, dating to the forties and fifties of the last century. On finding those old relics in a battered cardboard box, I was encouraged to start working on a book. This timely prodding came from some of my young well-wishers and friends such as architect Snehanshu and his wife Anisha, who is a scholar on the Red Fort. The famous Himalayan photographer Ashok Dilwali was extremely enthusiastic about this project and, like his father, BK Dilwali, fifty years ago, promised all possible help.

As I went on peering at many of my old negatives and slides with severe myopic eyes made worse by cataract, what came to my mind with a certain force was that while many of the photographs may be recognised and found interesting in future, all my mental images, including many of the important incidents and happenings in Delhi, were sure to be reduced to a handful of ashes if not written about soon.

This sudden urge to write about my impressions of Delhi also came from the fact that I had never kept any notes or a diary all my life. At best, some of my articles and features published long ago may be the only record about this historic city which I had seen from the young age of nine. But today, those features, too, might appear far from being detailed or complete.

That is how I began to put down my early impressions of Delhi, starting on a long train journey three years ago. Then, there was the difficult task of teaching myself to write cogently, and learning the intricacies of word-processing on a computer. For this I am grateful to my daughter Satarupa, who always kept me on the right track. The other person who had been kind enough to read my early efforts on Delhi was Ravi Dayal.

The noted historian, Professor Narayani Gupta, has really been the guiding spirit while I have struggled on with my efforts. The saddest part about writing this book on Delhi was that many of those friends, and near relatives, who have figured in this book are no longer there to see my work.

As for my wife Malabika, my readers would get an idea from the very first page to the last about my true feelings for her, spread over a period of nearly forty-five years. I would particularly like to mention my son-in-law, the architect Badri Narayanan, who not only cheered me on with his interesting remarks on my work, but also provided many rare books, as well as a satellite radio to reduce the drudgery of my single-handed efforts at word-processing. The names of many others who helped me along with this book are far too many to record here.

My father's well-known book, *Thy Hand Great Anarch!*, proved to be invaluable for cross-checking many socio-political facts. Here, I might just add that, in 1982, when he was writing those brilliant observations on Delhi, we used to discuss these often over a glass of vintage port at his hearthside at Oxford, and I consider myself blessed for that.

Dhruva N Chaudhuri
New Delhi, 2005